WILLIAM SHAKESPEARE

*

A MIDSUMMER NIGHT'S DREAM

EDITED BY
STANLEY WELLS

PENGUIN BOOKS

Penguin Books Ltd, Harmondsworth, Middlesex, England
Penguin Books, 40 West 23rd Street, New York, New York 10010, U.S.A.
Penguin Books Australia Ltd, Ringwood, Victoria, Australia
Penguin Books Canada Ltd, 2801 John Street, Markham, Ontario, Canada L3R 1B4
Penguin Books (N.Z.) Ltd, 182–190 Wairau Road, Auckland 10, New Zealand

—

This edition first published in Penguin Books 1967
Reprinted 1970, 1971, 1973, 1974, 1975, 1976, 1977, 1978 (twice),
1979, 1980, 1981, 1982 (twice), 1983

—

—

Made and printed in Great Britain
by Richard Clay (The Chaucer Press) Ltd,
Bungay, Suffolk
Set in Monotype Ehrhardt

CONTENTS

INTRODUCTION

DURING the interval of a performance – which was not going too well – of one of Shakespeare's other plays, I once heard a schoolboy say plaintively, 'I wish it was *A Midsummer Night's Dream*.' His was not a subtle form of theatre criticism; but the remark illustrates the affection in which this play is held, and the general confidence in its power to entertain. For many people it forms their first introduction to Shakespeare, whether in reading round the class or performance in village hall, school grounds, or professional theatre. And it continues to please many who would not normally enjoy a Shakespeare play. Much of its appeal comes from the scenes in which the 'mechanicals' – the rustic figures of Bully Bottom, Peter Quince, and their fellows – appear. These are among the few comic roles in Shakespeare which are quite often taken by professional comedians rather than 'straight' actors. The roles permit, and may gain from, the display of natural comic talent. A performer whose mere face is enough to set the audience laughing can do much with the silences of Bottom; a doleful clown can amuse and touch us in Moonshine's sad exasperation at his failure to persuade his stage-audience to take him seriously; the actor who plays Wall with blank inanity can give us amusement that does not spring directly from Shakespeare's lines.

Other parts of the play, too, can give theatrical pleasure of a kind that does not imply a sophisticated response. The fairy world provides the visual appeal of youthful figures moving with elegant stylization and costumed with delicacy

7

and charm. The forest scenes are apt to provoke designers to create richly romantic stage pictures. Music and dance are required by the action at various points, and can without too much violence be interpolated elsewhere. It is understandable that the most famous of all incidental music for Shakespeare should have been written for *A Midsummer Night's Dream*. Mendelssohn's exquisite score implies a particular style of production, a style that is now out-of-date. What modern producer would permit the introduction at the beginning of Act Five of a procession lasting as long as Mendelssohn's famous wedding march? Yet the quality of the music itself has been enough to provoke in our own time the reconstruction of the kind of presentation to which it would have been appropriate. Here the play was used as a setting for the music.

The variety of appeal inherent in *A Midsummer Night's Dream* is part of the source of its popularity, but has also caused it often to be reduced from its true stature. In the theatre it has been distorted by an over-emphasis on both its broad comedy and the opportunities it gives for stage spectacle. As early as 1661 was published *The Merry Conceited Humours of Bottom the Weaver*, in which the only characters other than the clowns are Oberon, Titania, Theseus, Hippolyta, and Puck. In Charles Johnson's *Love in a Forest* of 1723, an adaptation of *As You Like It*, the Pyramus and Thisbe episodes were incorporated as an entertainment for the banished Duke and his followers in the forest. America has seen a version called *Swinging the Dream* (1939), in which the Bottom who roared as gently as any sucking-dove was Louis Armstrong.

Over-exploitation of the play's opportunities for spectacle has too a long history. When Samuel Pepys saw it in 1662 only its incidental features appealed to him. He wrote in his diary: 'We saw *Midsummer Night's Dream*, which I had never seen before, nor shall ever again, for it is the most insipid ridiculous play that ever I saw in my life. I saw, I confess, some good dancing, and some handsome women, which was all my pleasure.' Thirty years later appeared *The Fairy Queen*, a lavish spectacle with a fine elaborate score by Henry Purcell. Though this is based on *A Midsummer Night's Dream*, Purcell set no line of Shakespeare. Another operatic version is Frederick Reynolds's (with music by Henry Bishop) of 1816, which provoked a violent attack by William Hazlitt. He wrote in a review:

'We have found to our cost, once for all, that the regions of fancy and the boards of Covent Garden are not the same thing. All that is fine in the play, was lost in the representation. The spirit was evaporated, the genius was fled; but the spectacle was fine: it was that which saved the play. Oh, ye scene-shifters, ye scene-painters, ye machinists and dress-makers, ye manufacturers of moon and stars that give no light, ye musical composers, ye men in the orchestra, fiddlers and trumpeters and players on the double drum and loud bassoon, rejoice! This is your triumph; it is not ours.'

He tells how, after seeing the performance, he read the play again and 'completely forgot all the noise we have heard and the sights we have seen'. He concluded that 'Poetry and the stage do not agree together.' The verdict is understandable from a critic of the time, when the play was presented in an unsympathetic adaptation performed in a vast theatre; but it is not permanently valid.

It was not till 1840 that the play was produced in something approximating to its original form. Samuel Phelps's production at Sadler's Wells in 1853 had great visual appeal, but seems nevertheless to have been a faithful attempt at least to translate into visual terms features that are a genuine part of the original play, rather than merely superimposing upon it extraneous spectacle. Later productions have not always avoided this danger. Shaw wrote of Augustin Daly's (1895):

'He certainly has no suspicion of the fact that every accessory he employs is brought in at the deadliest risk of destroying the magic spell woven by the poet. He swings Puck away on a clumsy trapeze with a ridiculous clash of the cymbals in the orchestra, in the fullest belief that he is thereby completing instead of destroying the effect of Puck's lines. His "panoramic illusion of the passage of Theseus's barge to Athens" is more absurd than anything that occurs in the tragedy of Pyramus and Thisbe in the last act.'

The pictorial, quasi-operatic style of production lasted well into this century, influencing for instance Max Reinhardt's film of 1935, but Harley Granville-Barker's Savoy Theatre performances in 1914 represented a thorough rethinking of the play which effected a healthy clearance of conventional accretions. Thus, Mendelssohn's music was abandoned in favour of English folk-tunes, and Puck and Oberon were no longer played by women, as had been the practice. Since Granville-Barker's time the desire for simplicity of presentation has slowly won ground over the desire for visual elaboration. The move has been assisted by the frequency of open-air performances, for which this play is particularly suitable. The development of the historical sense, at least in matters of theatrical taste, during the past hundred years has combined with studies of Shakespeare's verbal and theatrical artistry to encourage presentation of his plays in something approaching their own terms, rather than in adaptations that either grossly misrepresent their originals, or represent only a limited part of them. *A Midsummer Night's Dream* has benefited from this development. But the passage of time creates problems, and it is not surprising that producers frequently fail to maintain a total equilibrium in their presentation of Shakespeare's delicately balanced structure. It is some measure of the play's strength that it is almost infallibly entertaining under any circumstances; but inadequacies of presentation can cause us to underestimate the artistry with which it is composed. It is not simply by a happy accident that *A Midsummer Night's Dream* has retained for close on four centuries its power to entertain. Rather it is because this is a highly articulated structure, the product of a genius working with total mastery of his poetic and theatrical craft – a craft which was, of course, intimately bound up with the circumstances of the age.

The play was first printed in 1600. We do not know exactly when Shakespeare wrote it, though it is referred to in *Palladis Tamia*, a book by Francis Meres printed in 1598. It is generally thought of as more mature, and therefore probably later, than four other comedies – *The Two Gentlemen of Verona*, *The Taming of the Shrew*, *The Comedy of Errors*, and *Love's Labour's Lost*. These too cannot be firmly dated. *The Merchant of Venice*, also mentioned in Meres's book, is noticeably broader in range than *A Midsummer Night's Dream* (which is not to say that it is as assured a success in its own terms), and is reasonably thought of as later in date. Certainty would perhaps be most welcome as to whether *A Midsummer Night's Dream* came before or after *Romeo and Juliet*. It is tempting to imagine Shakespeare glancing at his own tragedy in the burlesque of *Pyramus and Thisbe*, with which it has features in common. This is a permissible speculation, but no more. The richness and complexity of *Romeo and Juliet* cause it to be more usually regarded as the later work.

Topical allusions have been sought in *A Midsummer Night's Dream*. Above all, Titania's lines (II.1.81–117) describing meteorological confusion have been taken as a reference to the bad summer of 1594. But bad summers were, we may suppose, no less common then than now. In any case, Titania speaks of unusually fine winters as well as bad summers; she is concerned with disorder in general. Her lines are thematically of high importance. To regard them as an attempt to win the audience's sympathy by causing her to drag in an irrelevant topical allusion is to take an insultingly low view of Shakespeare's artistry. It would be equally reasonable to argue that the lines were written in a year of perfectly normal weather in which they would have aroused no extra-dramatic response. The theatres were closed because of plague during most of 1593 and 1594. Probably *A Midsummer Night's Dream* was written either shortly before, during, or fairly soon after this period.

More important than the question of the play's exact date is the matter of whether, as has often been assumed, it was written for private performance on some particular occasion such as the marriage of a nobleman. Many attempts have been made to find a suitable wedding. Some of those who hold this theory patronize the play as an 'occasional' piece, commissioned for an audience of specialized taste. The suggestion has been offered that the play as we have it is a revision made for public performance, and even that Theseus and Hippolyta are 'stand-ins' for the pair whose wedding is supposed to have been celebrated. The belief that the wedding blessing of the last Act had some extra-dramatic significance encourages a loose assumption that it is superfluous, and has been used to justify its omission in performance. Interpretative arguments have been based upon the theory.

There is no outside evidence with any bearing on the matter. The theory has arisen from various features of the play itself. It is, certainly, much concerned with marriage; but so are many comedies. It ends with the fairies' blessing upon the married couples; but this is perfectly appropriate to Shakespeare's artistic scheme, and requires no other explanation. It includes a complimentary reference to Queen Elizabeth (II.1.157-8):

> *A certain aim he took*
> *At a fair vestal thronèd by the west. . . .*

Admittedly the Queen did not attend the public theatres; but an allusion to her does not imply that she was expected to be present at the play's first, or any other, performance. *A Midsummer Night's Dream* (like *Love's Labour's Lost*) appears to require an unusually large number of boy actors. Hippolyta, Hermia, Helena, Titania, Peaseblossom, Cobweb, Moth, and Mustardseed would all have been boys' parts. Puck and Oberon too may have been played by boys or young men. But the title page of the first edition, printed in 1600, tells us that the play was 'sundry times publicly acted by the Right Honourable the Lord Chamberlain his servants'. If Shakespeare's company could at any time muster enough boys for public performances, we have no reason to doubt that it could have done so from the start. Thus the suggestion that the roles of the fairies were intended to be taken by children of the hypothetical noble house seems purely whimsical. The stage directions of the first edition, which was probably printed from Shakespeare's manuscript, show no essential differences from those in his other plays; a direction such as '*Enter a* Fairie *at one doore, and* Robin goodfellow *at another*' (II.1.0) suggests that he had in mind the structure of the public theatres. Furthermore, although noble weddings in Shakespeare's time were sometimes graced with formal entertainments, usually of the nature of a masque, the first play certainly known to have been written for such an occasion is Samuel Daniel's *Hymen's Triumph*. This was performed in 1614, some twenty years after the composition of *A Midsummer Night's Dream*. By this time the tradition of courtly entertainments had developed greatly; and *Hymen's Triumph* does not appear to have been played in a public theatre.

To me, then, it seems credible that *A Midsummer Night's Dream* was always intended for the public theatres.

A Midsummer Night's Dream is one of the small group of plays in which Shakespeare appears not to have depended upon already existing narrative material. Whereas in *The Comedy of Errors*, for example, he worked from a Latin comedy (Plautus's *Menaechmi*), and in *As You Like It* he was to dramatize an English prose tale (Thomas Lodge's *Rosalind*), we know of nothing that would have provided the main story of *A Midsummer Night's Dream*. In this, as in other respects, it is one of his most individual creations. Inevitably, however, his reading played some part in its genesis. He could have read about Theseus and Hippolyta in the first few pages of Sir Thomas North's great translation (first published in 1579) of Plutarch's *Lives of the Noble Grecians and Romans*, later to become one of his most important source works. He may also have found a few hints about the same characters in Chaucer's *The Knight's Tale*. But he can scarcely be said to have gleaned more than the names and a few general suggestions for characterization from these sources. Similarly with Oberon: the old romance of *Huon of Bordeaux* gave him a few hints, no more. Titania's name seems to have come from Ovid's *Metamorphoses*, where it is used as an adjective for more than one goddess descended of the Titans. Shakespeare knew his Ovid well, in both Latin and English. Several details of the play are influenced by the *Metamorphoses*, and Shakespeare's whole treatment of the Pyramus and Thisbe story may have been sparked off by his reading of it in Arthur Golding's translation of Ovid, published in 1567. The verse medium is that of the fourteener, which often results in a drab, monotonous style. Golding's lines almost parody themselves:

The wall that parted house from house had riven therein a
*   cranny*
Which shrunk at making of the wall; this fault not marked of
*   any*
Of many hundred years before (what doth not love espy!)
These lovers first of all found out, and made a way whereby
To talk together secretly, and through the same did go
Their loving whisperings very light and safely to and fro.

Finding Thisbe's mantle stained with blood, Pyramus thinks she is dead:

And when he had bewept and kissed the garment which he
*   knew,*
'Receive thou my blood too,' quoth he, and therewithal he drew
His sword, the which among his guts he thrust, and by and by
Did draw it from the bleeding wound beginning for to die,
And cast himself upon his back. The blood did spin on high
As when a conduit pipe is cracked, the water bursting out
Doth shoot itself a great way off and pierce the air about.

15

Then Thisbe, alive after all, comes upon her dying lover, crying:

'Alas, what chance, my Pyramus, hath parted thee and me?
Make answer, O my Pyramus; it is thy Thisb', even she
Whom thou dost love most heartily, that speaketh unto thee.
Give ear and raise thy heavy head.' He, hearing Thisbe's
     name,
Lift up his dying eyes, and having seen her closed the same.
But when she knew her mantle there and saw his scabbard lie
Without the sword : 'Unhappy man, thy love hath made thee
     die.'

This tale was very popular in the late sixteenth century. Many versions of it written in the sort of poetic style that must have seemed old-fashioned in the 1590s have survived, and Shakespeare probably read several of them in preparation for his own dramatization of the story.

There are a number of writings which may have suggested Bottom's translation into an ass, just as there are others which may have provided details for the portrayal of the fairy world, but it is difficult to pinpoint precise sources.

One of the most prominent characteristics of Shakespeare's playwriting career is a constant striving not to repeat himself, at any rate in essentials. Each of his plays creates its own world. At the same time, there are close relationships between many of them. He seems to have enjoyed playing variations on a theme, making use of similar material in different ways. Part of the background of *A Midsummer Night's Dream* is his own *Love's Labour's Lost*, written only a short time before. Both are highly patterned plays, concerning the exploits in wooing of pairs of lovers. Both reach their climax in an entertainment given by characters of the sub-plot for the benefit of their social superiors. In both plays the entertainments are punctuated by sarcastic comments from their stage audiences. The link between the plays, and a difference between them, is pointed by a verbal echo. 'Our wooing doth not end like an old play,' says Berowne in *Love's Labour's Lost*; 'Jack hath not Jill.' The happy ending of *A Midsummer Night's Dream* is foretold by Puck (III.2.461–3) with

> *Jack shall have Jill;*
> *Naught shall go ill.*
> *The man shall have his mare again, and all shall be well.*

No doubt Shakespeare was conscious of the relationship. But it would be false to suggest that the later play was simply a more successful attempt to do something which had not quite come off in the earlier. Each is successful in its own way, and the differences between them are as important as the resemblances. It is worth noticing that for *Love's Labour's Lost*, as for *A Midsummer Night's Dream*, there is no known main source. The other play of which this is true is *The Tempest*, which has significant resemblances to *A Midsummer Night's Dream*.

In *A Midsummer Night's Dream* Shakespeare was concerned to create characters that would serve his own purposes, not to portray historical or mythical figures. It would be false to stress Theseus's origins in classical legend. Shakespeare uses the classical hero's name, and a few of his attributes, giving him the medieval title of Duke (instead of King) of Athens. Theseus carries with him some suggestion of the classical world, with his dignified manner, his references to his kinsman Hercules, and the allusions to his love affairs. Yet to the Elizabethan audience he cannot have been far removed from a nobleman – perhaps a duke – of their own times. The opening scene shows him (like Timon of Athens in the first scene of his play) exercising the function of a benevolent landlord called upon to solve his tenants' personal problems. Nor has his Hippolyta many of the characteristics of a Queen of the Amazons. Shakespeare gives them enough non-Elizabethan traits to suggest a certain ideal quality, but leaves them as figures that would in essentials be recognizable to his audience. They have a maturity and self-command which set them off from the young lovers.

The young people are not far removed in social standing from the Duke and Duchess. The Duke knows something of their affairs before the play begins, and at the wedding festivities their easy sharing in their host's conversation suggests no awe of him. And the workmen (or mechanicals), obviously on a much lower level of society, associate them with the Duke and Duchess: 'Masters,' says Snug (IV.2. 15–16), 'the Duke is coming from the temple, and there is two or three lords and ladies more married.' The characterization of the young people is deliberately slight. Shakespeare is not anxious to suggest particularity; they are representative figures, practically interchangeable, as the play's action shows. In the theatre, of course, their anonymity is less noticeable than in reading.

Oberon and Titania, too, are of calculatedly mixed origin. Oberon smacks of medieval romance: he wants the changeling boy to be a 'Knight of his train, to trace the forests wild' (II.1.25). Both he and Titania are more than once associated with India, which adds an exotic touch. They are also strongly reminiscent of classical deities, though no precise identification is suggested. Both have had love affairs with mortals, and Titania has had a human 'votaress' of her order – the mother of her changeling boy. The exact nature of their power is left uncertain; but it is considerable. Their dissension is responsible for the disorder of the seasons. On the whole they exercise their power for beneficent ends, and there is a sense in which they are projections of forces of nature favourable to humanity just as their human counterparts, Theseus and Hippolyta, exercise a benevolent rule over the citizens of Athens.

Oberon and Titania appear to be thought of as a fully-grown man and woman. Their attendants, however, are imagined as tiny creatures, able to creep into acorn cups, and in danger of being drowned if a bee's honey bag breaks. Their tininess is something that Shakespeare derived from traditional beliefs and to which, both here and in the Queen Mab speech in *Romeo and Juliet*, he gave such memorable expression as to start a literary tradition that still survives. That the fairies cannot be thus represented on the stage is not merely obvious; it is also a point of some importance in the scheme of the play. Shakespeare seems deliberately to draw attention to the discrepancies between what we see and what is described. Here the audience is required to use its imagination in order to make the play possible. The same is true of the stage audience in the final scene. The other inhabitant of the play's fairy world, Robin Goodfellow, or Puck, was a well-known figure in folk-lore, though Shakespeare adds some hints of the classical Mercury. Obviously he is without the ethereal quality of the Fairy King and Queen's attendants. As Oberon's agent his function is ultimately beneficent, but he has an independent love of mischief. His characteristics are described in the dialogue between himself and a fairy in Act Two, Scene One.

The other group of characters, the workmen or mechanicals, Shakespeare makes no attempt to portray as Athenians, though he gives his actors ample scope for individual characterization. As with the fairies, he lightly exploits the discrepancy between what we hear and what we see: the 'hard-handed men of Athens' are countrymen of England, through and through. To his original audience they would have suggested a group of amateur actors, perhaps with ambitions of turning professional, such as flourished some twenty or thirty years before the play was written. There are six actors in Peter Quince's company, and this would have been a normal number in a popular troupe of the mid sixteenth century. It is the plays such as these troupes performed that are burlesqued in the last Act.

Shakespeare introduces his groups of characters and organizes his narrative material with great skill. The matter of the opening interchange, between Theseus and Hippolyta, indicates the course the play is to take, looking forward to its culmination in marriage and celebration. These noble lovers provide a comparatively static framework for the play. After this opening episode, they will not reappear till the first scene of Act Four. Their relationship with each other is to remain constant, suggesting a basis of maturity and common sense which serves as a foil to the instability of the young lovers. The nature of their relationship, ardent but controlled, is suggested in the play's opening lines in terms of the normal operation of nature:

> *Four days will quickly steep themselves in night ;*
> *Four nights will quickly dream away the time :*
> *And then the moon – like to a silver bow*
> *New-bent in heaven – shall behold the night*
> *Of our solemnities.*

The swift purposefulness of the style establishes a mood of harmony and pleasurable anticipation. Stress is laid already on the moon, an image whose recurrence will help to create the play's unity of poetic style. It sheds its radiance throughout, lingering Theseus's desires, beholding the night of his solemnities, providing a setting for the meeting of the Fairy King and Queen, quenching Cupid's arrow in its beams, looking with a watery eye upon Titania and Bottom, and making a personal appearance in the interlude of Pyramus and Thisbe.

Into this opening harmony comes a harsh interruption. Hermia is at odds with her father. Theseus presents her an alternative if she continues to refuse to obey; and he does so in terms of natural imagery:

> *Either to die the death, or to abjure*
> *For ever the society of men. . . .*
> *Thrice blessèd they that master so their blood*
> *To undergo such maiden pilgrimage ;*
> *But earthlier happy is the rose distilled*
> *Than that which, withering on the virgin thorn,*
> *Grows, lives, and dies in single blessedness.*

When Hermia and Lysander are left alone, the same image recurs:

> *How now, my love? Why is your cheek so pale?*
> *How chance the roses there do fade so fast?*

The situation as it stands could issue in either tragedy (as a similar situation does in *Romeo and Juliet*) or comedy. As he is here choosing comedy, Shakespeare adopts a style that does not involve us too closely in the lovers' emotions. But he gives it enough body, enough reference to larger concepts, both to keep our sympathetic interest and to enable us to see the lovers' dilemma as an image of universal human experience. It is important to establish such a sympathy early, before the farcical confusions develop, so Lysander is given a lyrical expression of the fragility of love:

> Or if there were a sympathy in choice,
> War, death, or sickness did lay siege to it,
> Making it momentany as a sound,
> Swift as a shadow, short as any dream,
> Brief as the lightning in the collied night,
> That in a spleen unfolds both heaven and earth,
> And – ere a man hath power to say 'Behold!' –
> The jaws of darkness do devour it up.
> So quick bright things come to confusion.

There is pathos here; even a hint of the possibility of tragedy. The same imagery recurs in a premonitory passage in *Romeo and Juliet* (II.2.117–20), where Juliet says:

> I have no joy of this contract tonight.
> It is too rash, too unadvised, too sudden;
> Too like the lightning, which doth cease to be
> Ere one can say 'It lightens'.

Yet Lysander's lines are not out of place in a romantic comedy, because they are generalized: a reflection on what might be rather than what is – and because soon after them he brings forward a plan by which he and Hermia may get out of their difficult situation. They will leave Athens and make for his widowed aunt's house, seven leagues away. And they will meet 'in the wood, a league without the town'.

Helena's entrance gives scope for a comically touching demonstration of her jealousy. Her soliloquy which closes the scene states an important idea, already hinted at, with which Shakespeare is to be concerned: the irrationality of love, the tension between what people ought reasonably to feel and what in fact they do feel. Demetrius, she says,

> ... errs, doting on Hermia's eyes,
> So I, admiring of his qualities.

Things base and vile, holding no quantity,
Love can transpose to form and dignity.

We may remember this later, especially when we see Bottom adored by Titania. Helena goes on to speak of the irrationality of love, suggesting a dislocation between the eyes and the mind, in which however the eyes are regarded as the objective force.

Love looks not with the eyes, but with the mind,
And therefore is winged Cupid painted blind.
Nor hath love's mind of any judgement taste;
Wings and no eyes figure unheedy haste.
And therefore is love said to be a child
Because in choice he is so oft beguiled.

The first scene, then, has introduced us to two related sets of characters – the Duke and Duchess and the young lovers – and set the romantic plot in motion by presenting the conflict between the young people and their elders. Helena ends the scene with a threat of treachery to Hermia and Lysander. She will reveal their plot to Demetrius, who will then pursue Hermia to the wood.

The second scene, which introduces the mechanicals, also opens by looking forward to the end of the play, as Peter Quince shows 'the scroll of every man's name which is thought fit through all Athens to play in our interlude before the Duke and the Duchess on his wedding day at night.' The interlude will concern characters resembling those we have just seen: young lovers whose romance is thwarted by parental opposition. Roles are decided, parts distributed, and the actors arrange to meet the next night for a rehearsal – in the wood.

With the third scene (Act Two, Scene One) we reach the wood, which has its own function in the play. As in, for instance, *As You Like It*, and even a play as different from *A Midsummer Night's Dream* as *King Lear*, the movement from town to country, from the control of organized society to the freedom of nature, is appropriate to the emotional experiences of the persons involved. The wood is a place of liberation, of reassessment, leading through a stage of disorganization to a finally increased stability. Here we meet the remaining group of characters. Oberon and Titania's mutual recriminations recall the jealousies of the mortal lovers. Again we have a pointer to the last Act – this time to the very end of the play: Titania is jealous that Oberon has come all the way from India only because his 'warrior love' Hippolyta is marrying Theseus, and Oberon wishes 'To give their bed joy and prosperity'. Titania defends herself against Oberon's jealous accusations in the great speech beginning 'These are the forgeries of jealousy'. Most of it has no relevance to the plot, nor is it important in characterizing Titania. It is sometimes thought of as no more than an extended topical reference. It can also be regarded simply as a piece of poetry – Shakespeare indulging his poetic talent at the expense of the drama. The speech has, of course, great poetic merit, and gives the audience pleasure in its own right. If this were its only point it would be expendable; and indeed it has often been severely cut in performance. But to dismiss it as irrelevant, or as mere decoration, is to fail to give proper allowance to the nature of poetic drama. Several major speeches in this play are important not because they further the action or elaborate a character, but because they represent an explicit verbal development of ideas hinted at in other parts of the play. They are as it were arias in which snatches of melody heard elsewhere are fully developed. Titania's lines present a poetic image of confusion in the world of nature, occasioned by Oberon's attacks upon herself and her followers.

The 'distemperature' in nature is such that 'The seasons alter'. Behind this lies a notion of the proper order of things, based on the rhythm of the seasons and the workings of nature. The fairy characters have a specially close relationship with nature. They are the wood-dwellers. They have a function as guardians of things natural. They are frequently associated with flowers – 'I know a bank where the wild thyme blows . . .', says Oberon (II.1.249); and the first fairy to enter is busy hanging pearls in cowslips' ears. The disruption in the natural order of things which we see in Titania's speech is caused by the quasi-human passions of the fairies. In this respect the speech may be seen as an image of the construction and movement of the whole play. Many other things relate to it. Just as the quarrel between these lovers causes confusion in the seasons, so later (II.1.231–3) Helena (in more comic terms) will represent her pursuit of the man she loves by a similar reversal:

> *Apollo flies, and Daphne holds the chase;*
> *The dove pursues the griffin; the mild hind*
> *Makes speed to catch the tiger. . . .*

Titania's speech is without any comic tinge, though (like Lysander's lines mentioned earlier) it is rendered appropriate to a comedy by its generalized, somewhat distancing style. It presents seriously the danger of disaster when control is lost and the malevolent forces of nature gain the upper hand. The presence of such forces is frequently suggested. Quick bright things can come to confusion. The fairies sing (II.2.22–3):

> *Beetles black, approach not near,*
> *Worm nor snail, do no offence.*

25

Hermia dreams that a serpent is eating her heart away. Oberon and his fellows are contrasted (III.2.386–7) with the spirits who

> *wilfully themselves exile from light,*
> *And must for aye consort with black-browed night . . .*

and Oberon's final benediction is also an exorcism of 'the blots of nature's hand'.

Titania and Oberon part, still in enmity, and he prepares his plot to avenge his wrong. The character groups of the play begin to interact. For the first time we see two of the lovers – Helena and Demetrius – in the wood; and we have an immediate hint of some of the irrationality of what is going to happen there in Demetrius's pun (II.1.192) on an Elizabethan sense of 'wood', which could also mean 'mad'; he is

> *wood within this wood*
> *Because I cannot meet my Hermia.*

Shakespeare uses the flower that Puck fetches as the linking force between the plots; for Oberon decides that besides dropping some of the juice on Titania's eyes, he will have Puck drop some of it too upon Demetrius's, making him requite Helena's passion. In fact Puck anoints Lysander's eyes and he falls madly in love with Helena. Ironically he attributes this new affection to his reason (II.2.121–8), whereas we know that the change has been effected by Puck's juice.

> *The will of man is by his reason swayed,*
> *And reason says you are the worthier maid.*
> *Things growing are not ripe until their season;*
> *So I, being young, till now ripe not to reason.*
> *And touching now the point of human skill,*
> *Reason becomes the marshal to my will,*

And leads me to your eyes, where I o'erlook
Love's stories written in love's richest book.

We shall remember the antithesis between love and reason at a later point.

The comic confusions of the lovers are caused by the failure of their reason to keep pace with their emotions. They are in an adolescent whirl. Under the spell of an illusion, they – very understandably – mistake it for reality. Now (Act Three, Scene One) in the midst of their troubles come the mechanicals to rehearse their play. They are in somewhat similar case. They are attempting to cope with a world of illusion, the stage presentation of the classical legend of Pyramus and Thisbe. It is not a world in which they feel comfortable. They too are unable to distinguish between the imaginary and the real, and they fear that others will share their inability. Lion must tell the audience that he is really Snug the joiner; Bottom must explain that he is not really killed as Pyramus. Their confusions find expression in a way similar to those of the lovers. Puck's juice, applied to the lovers' eyes, distorts their point of view. In the forthcoming scene in the forest where the confusion is at its height, Demetrius and Lysander cannot see each other, and are misled by Puck into thinking they hear each other's voice. The mechanicals, too, have their senses confused; 'he goes but to see a noise that he heard', says Quince of Pyramus; Bottom, as he awakes, becomes similarly muddled. In the last Act Pyramus says:

I see a voice. Now will I to the chink
To spy an I can hear my Thisbe's face . . .

and Bottom invites his audience either to see an epilogue or hear a dance. The notion of a dislocation between the senses, and between the senses and the brain, is recurrent.

Throughout the play Shakespeare brilliantly reconciles opposites.

> *How shall we find the concord of this discord?*

asks Theseus (V.1.60); Shakespeare shows us. Classical Athens is brought into contact with sixteenth-century Warwickshire. The dignity of Theseus and Hippolyta co-exists with the youthful silliness of the younger lovers. Verse in a style of the most delicate fantasy is juxtaposed with comic prose of earthy robustness. Hard-handed working men enact a classical story of tragic love. The climax of this method comes when the ethereal Titania, who had been lulled to sleep by the lullaby of her attendant fairies, is aroused by Bottom's rustic song. He is now literally asinine. But under the influence of Puck's magic juice she is enthralled. Her ear and eye are both enamoured. Even Bottom, fool that he is, and metamorphosed into an ass, can see that her love for him is unreasonable; but he is not such a fool as to reject it:

TITANIA
> *I pray thee, gentle mortal, sing again!*
> *Mine ear is much enamoured of thy note.*
> *So is mine eye enthrallèd to thy shape,*
> *And thy fair virtue's force perforce doth move me*
> *On the first view to say, to swear, I love thee.*

BOTTOM *Methinks, mistress, you should have little reason for that. And yet, to say the truth, reason and love keep little company together nowadays – the more the pity that some honest neighbours will not make them friends.*

> III.1.130–38

The comedy of Bottom and Titania is of the sort most admired by Sir Philip Sidney, in which there is both laughter and delight. In *An Apology for Poetry*, of about 1581-3, Sidney wrote:

Delight hath a joy in it, either permanent or present. Laughter hath only a scornful tickling . . . for as in Alexander's picture well set out we delight without laughter, and in twenty mad antics we laugh without delight ; so in Hercules, painted with his great beard and furious countenance, in woman's attire, spinning at Omphale's commandment, it breedeth both delight and laughter. For the representing of so strange a power in love procureth delight : and the scornfulness of the action stirreth laughter.

Shakespeare might almost have been playing a deliberate variation upon the situation portrayed by Sidney.

The first edition of this play has no Act divisions, and it seems unlikely that Shakespeare, as he wrote, had an act-structure in mind. The scenes flow smoothly into each other till the end of that between Titania and Bottom (III.1). Here there is a natural break. The next scene begins with something of a recapitulatory episode; for a few moments the dialogue, between Oberon and Puck, looks back upon the preceding action. Then the plot involving the lovers is resumed. In the subsequent episode Hermia speaks significantly of the effect of night on the senses:

Dark night that from the eye his function takes
The ear more quick of apprehension makes.
Wherein it doth impair the seeing sense
It pays the hearing double recompense.
Thou art not by mine eye, Lysander, found ;
Mine ear – I thank it – brought me to thy sound.

The stage is set for the full exploitation of the lovers' confusions, and Shakespeare develops the situation with fertile invention. The action has not quite reached the point of maximum complexity when Oberon gives Puck the instruction that shows us how the resolution is to be effected:

> Then crush this herb into Lysander's eye –
> Whose liquor hath this virtuous property,
> To take from thence all error with his might,
> And make his eyeballs roll with wonted sight.
> When they next wake, all this derision
> Shall seem a dream and fruitless vision. . . .

The night is ending, and Puck and Oberon forecast the approach of day in a passage of poetic expansiveness (III.2.378–93) which superbly effects a transition of mood. Puck brings the lovers together, sends them to sleep, and squeezes the herb on Lysander's eyes. That the movement of the play is gradually changing direction is further subtly indicated by the fact that each of the lovers, falling asleep, speaks of the approach of day. When Titania and Bottom too fall asleep in each other's arms the action has reached its most complex moment. Oberon begins to feel pity for Titania, who has given up to him the changeling boy. He instructs Puck to remove Bottom's ass's head, and himself releases Titania from her spell. To the sound of music the Fairy King and Queen are reconciled, and the symbolic significance of their reunion is emphasized by the dance with which it is celebrated. Again we look forward to the events to come:

> Now thou and I are new in amity,
> And will tomorrow midnight solemnly
> Dance in Duke Theseus' house triumphantly,
> And bless it to all fair prosperity.

The reconciliation of Oberon and Titania makes possible the clarification of the lovers' problems. The night is ending. Day approaches, and with it there re-enter the play's symbols of sanity and maturity – Theseus and Hippolyta, who have been celebrating a rite of May in the early morning. Their entrance is marked by another poetic passage of more than immediate significance. They are going to enjoy hearing the baying of their pack of dogs

> *matched in mouth like bells,*
> *Each under each.*

It is the theme of concord, the notion of a harmony which permits the existence of diversity. It is a symbol of the possibility of a unity that is not sameness, an agreement that can include disagreement:

> *So musical a discord, such sweet thunder.*

And before us is an emblem of at least the temporary existence of such a concord, as the four lovers, last seen in violent rivalry, sleep quietly close by each other. Theseus, having them woken by his hunting horns, points the paradox:

> *I know you two are rival enemies.*
> *How comes this gentle concord in the world,*
> *That hatred is so far from jealousy*
> *To sleep by hate, and fear no enmity?*

As the two young men explain themselves to the Duke, it becomes clear that their problems are nearing a solution. Demetrius's love for Hermia is 'Melted as the snow'; now he loves Helena. So she is satisfied. And Egeus's renewed objections to the marriage of Lysander and Hermia are authoritatively overcome by Theseus. The bewildering confusions of the dream are dissolving into a satisfying order of reality. The lovers, left together, give expression to their sense of wonder in a passage (IV.1.186–98) remarkable for a poetic quality deriving from an awareness of the tension between illusion and reality, between the visions of dreamland and the facts of the morning light.

> *These things seem small and undistinguishable,*
> *Like far-off mountains turnèd into clouds . . .*

says Demetrius, formulating a curious characteristic of the play, which itself has the quality of something looked at from a distance. It is an effect at once of the jewelled delicacy of its style, its controlled neatness of structure, the sense in the fairy scenes of great distances rapidly traversed, and also perhaps of the many passages in which characters describe events of the past: passages such as Titania's description (II.1.123–37) of her friendship with the changeling boy's mother, and Oberon's about the time when Cupid shot his arrow at the imperial votaress (II.1.148–68).

The lovers' feeling of wonder includes a sense of relief that a bad dream is over, and their problems are solved. But Oberon and Puck have made possible another wakening into reality: Bottom's. It might have seemed less desirable than that which precedes it. Bottom's was a pleasant dream: 'a most rare vision' translating him from mundane reality into an ideal world of love and beauty. For him, as for Caliban in *The Tempest*, the clouds have opened and shown riches. Bottom might well have anticipated Caliban also in crying to dream again. Yet he does not regret his awakening, but rather endears himself to us by the typical dislocations in his savouring of it: 'The eye of man hath not heard, the ear of man hath not seen, man's hand is not able to taste, his tongue to conceive, nor his heart to report what my dream was!' His speech of awakening is as masterly a piece of prose as the lovers' episode is of verse; and his irruption into the company of his fellows,

32

grieving over his absence, is a great moment for the actor.

By now all the complications of the plot are resolved. But the play is not over. From the start we have been kept aware that it is to culminate in marriage, celebration, and benediction. We know too that the tragedy of Pyramus and Thisbe has yet to be enacted. The impetus that carries us forward into the final scenes is that of expectation, not of plot tension. Before the celebrations begin we are allowed a moment of reflection as Theseus and Hippolyta think over what 'these lovers' speak of. To Hippolyta it seems strange; to Theseus, 'More strange than true.' In another speech of poetic recapitulation he compares the imaginations of lovers with those of madmen and poets. All of them are apt to confuse the illusory with the real. This is a splendid expression of a point of view which it would be unwise to identify with Shakespeare's. There is something scoffing and dismissive in Theseus's attitude; he is here the plain, blunt man who prides himself on knowing what's what, on the exercise of 'cool reason'. Hippolyta supplies the necessary corrective:

> But all the story of the night told over,
> And all their minds transfigured so together,
> More witnesseth than fancy's images,
> And grows to something of great constancy;
> But howsoever, strange and admirable.

She can conceive what the lovers have been through; and her use of the word 'transfigured' helps to suggest that the woodland scenes represent for them a genuine shaping experience. Looked at coldly, the adventures of the night are simply a mechanical set of misunderstandings, which to Theseus seem like a complete delusion. But Hippolyta is struck by the fact that 'all their minds' were affected.

She can see some hint of a power beyond that of fancy. Unlike Theseus, Hippolyta, or indeed the lovers, we of the audience have seen into the fairy world that has been influencing human actions, and can sympathize with Hippolyta. We are, too, made to feel that the events of the night have been a significant experience for the lovers, teaching them something about themselves; that they come out of the wood more mature than when they went into it. It is difficult to rationalize this impression. The change in Demetrius's attitude to Helena has been brought about by purely external means. No profound psychological process has been portrayed. The lovers' wanderings in the wood have occupied only one night. But it has been an enchanted, timeless night. As the lovers go off to marriage, we are likely to feel that they have been through a necessary but profoundly disturbing experience, and that now they are safely on the other side of it. The experience has grown 'to something of great constancy', enriching their lives just as Bottom's 'rare vision' enriches his. They bring back into the ordinary world something that they learned in the world of imagination. The illusory has its part in the total experience of reality.

The performance that Bottom and his fellows give before the wedding couples is of course marvellously funny. Shakespeare's verbal virtuosity here is employed in the art of parody, and his target is the interludes, which mixed human characters with personifications, and which flourished two or three decades before he was writing. Those decades had seen a phenomenal development in verse style, and the old modes were ripe for mockery. But these episodes have their place too in the more serious scheme of the play. We have seen already that the lovers needed the tolerance and understanding indulgence of other people to achieve their happiness. The play scene extends this idea outside the world of the lovers to other groups of society too. Theseus is clearly warned that the mechanicals' play is 'nothing, nothing in the world', but insists that he will hear it, since

> *never anything can be amiss*
> *When simpleness and duty tender it.*

The suggestion that for us the interest of the performance should lie partly in the relationship between the amateur actors and their audience is given in Theseus's lines beginning 'The kinder we, to give them thanks for nothing.' He is willing to give credit to his subjects for their good intentions even if the result is not very successful:

> *And what poor duty cannot do, noble respect*
> *Takes it in might, not merit.*

He is willing, in fact, to exert his imagination in the attempt to pierce to the reality behind illusory appearances, to find the 'concord of this discord' (V.i.60). He shows here something of the understanding that previously seemed to belong rather to Hippolyta. The shift in attitudes is interesting. Shakespeare seems to be hinting at the infinite adjustments necessary in the establishment of social and emotional harmony.

The performance of the interlude itself shows literal-minded men trying to cope with a world of illusion, and failing to do so. The discrepancy is so severe that the performance might well have seemed silly, were it not rescued by our knowledge of the good intentions of the performers, and our predisposition to make allowances for them. But the line between charitable acceptance and exasperated rejection is thin, and there are times when the stage-audience is in danger of crossing it:

HIPPOLYTA *This is the silliest stuff that ever I heard.*

THESEUS *The best in this kind are but shadows; and the worst are no worse, if imagination amend them.*

HIPPOLYTA *It must be your imagination, then, and not theirs.*

THESEUS *If we imagine no worse of them than they of themselves, they may pass for excellent men.*

The performance continues with other comments, not all complimentary, from the stage-audience. Fiasco is prevented only by the imaginative indulgence of the spectators, which never seems at all sentimental, since Shakespeare gives a cutting edge to many of their comments.

The play's last scene, then, is not a mere comic appendage. Rather does it serve as an emblem of both the possibility and the precariousness of happiness in human relationships; of the fact that this can be achieved only through a constant openness of the imagination, by the exercise of a charitable understanding, a willingness to accept people as they are rather than rejecting them for their inadequacies, even if this means feeding what one knows to be their illusions. We all pass for excellent men by what we imagine of ourselves. The scene becomes a dancing vision of an achieved unity, a musical discord. Like the baying of the hounds in Theseus's pack, each voice has full expression, moving freely and joyously in a passage of perfect counterpoint. The actors of the interlude need the imaginative participation of their stage-audience if they are to succeed. This is as true of the play itself as of the play within the play. It is all unreal; yet, if we too bring our imaginations to it, it may grow to something of great constancy, a universal harmony, a music of the spheres in which each sings its own song. On these images

of concord – the marriage festivity, the dance, the music –
the forces of nature shower their blessings:

> *So shall all the couples three*
> *Ever true in loving be. . . .*

It remains only for Puck to suggest to the real audience
that it too has a part to perform. If the spectators have
disliked the play they need regard it as no more than an
illusion, a dream action performed by shadows. But if they
have enjoyed it they can confer a sort of reality upon the
poet's and the actors' world, and make their contact with it:

> *Give me your hands if we be friends,*
> *And Robin shall restore amends.*

FURTHER READING

Background material

E. K. Chambers has an article 'On the Occasion of *A Mid-
summer Night's Dream*' (1916, reprinted in *Shakespearian
Gleanings*, 1946). W. J. Lawrence states the case against the
theory that this is a wedding-play in 'A Plummet for Bottom's
Dream' (1922, reprinted in *Shakespeare's Workshop*, Oxford,
1928). The edition by Sir Arthur Quiller-Couch and John
Dover Wilson (Cambridge, 1924 etc.) includes Quiller-Couch's
introduction, Dover Wilson's discussion of the text, and Harold
Child's summary of the stage history. Harold F. Brooks's new
Arden edition (1979) has a long introduction and a valuably
detailed commentary. Sources are discussed in Kenneth Muir's
The Sources of Shakespeare's Plays (1977); Geoffrey Bullough
reprints and discusses sources and analogues in *Narrative and
Dramatic Sources of Shakespeare*, Vol. 1 (1957). Background to
the fairies is provided by M. W. Latham in *The Elizabethan
Fairies* (New York, 1930), and K. M. Briggs in *The Anatomy of
Puck* (1959). They are more critically discussed in Ernest
Schanzer's 'The Moon and the Fairies in *A Midsummer Night's
Dream*' (*University of Toronto Quarterly* XXIV, 3, April 1955).
J. W. Robinson's 'Palpable Hot Ice: Dramatic Burlesque in *A
Midsummer Night's Dream*' (*Studies in Philology* LXI, No. 2,
Part 1, April 1964) is a helpful examination of the targets and
methods of burlesque in the Pyramus and Thisbe episodes.

Criticism

Harley Granville-Barker's Preface to the Players' Shakespeare
edition (1924) is reprinted in his *Prefaces to Shakespeare*, Vol.
VI (1974). Enid Welsford has a section on the play in *The Court
Masque* (1927). G. Wilson Knight, in *The Shakespearian
Tempest* (1932), approaches it mainly through an examination

39

of its imagery. M. C. Bradbrook has some perceptive comments in *Shakespeare and Elizabethan Poetry* (1951). Georges A. Bonnard's 'Shakespeare's Purpose in *A Midsummer Night's Dream*' (*Shakespeare Jahrbuch*, XCII, 1956) is particularly good on the relationship between the mechanicals and the lovers. Paul A. Olson's '*A Midsummer Night's Dream* and the Meaning of Court Marriage' (*ELH*, XXIV, 1957) is an interpretation, conducted with much learning, based on the 'wedding-play' theory. John Russell Brown (*Shakespeare and his Comedies*, 1957), C. L. Barber (*Shakespeare's Festive Comedy*, Princeton, 1959), Bertrand Evans (*Shakespeare's Comedies*, 1960), Glynne Wickham (*Shakespeare's Dramatic Heritage*, 1969), and Alexander Leggatt (*Shakespeare's Comedy of Love*, 1974) all have variously interesting chapters on the play. W. M. Merchant, in '*A Midsummer Night's Dream*, a visual recreation' (*Early Shakespeare*, Stratford-upon-Avon Studies, 3, 1961), is much concerned with the history of its presentation on the stage. Peter Brook's famous Stratford-upon-Avon production (1970) is discussed in two articles in *Shakespeare Survey 24* (1971), and an acting edition of it has been edited by Glenn Loney (Chicago, 1974). There are brief but suggestive sections on the play in Frank Kermode's 'The Mature Comedies' (*Early Shakespeare*, Stratford-upon-Avon Studies, 3, 1961), G. K. Hunter's *Shakespeare: The Late Comedies* (1962), and Nevill Coghill's *Shakespeare's Professional Skills* (Cambridge, 1964). David P. Young has written a valuable full-length study called *Something of Great Constancy: The Art of 'A Midsummer Night's Dream'* (1966), and Stephen Fender's *Shakespeare: 'A Midsummer Night's Dream'* (Arnold's Studies in English Literature, No. 35, 1968) is a thoughtful short book about the play.

A MIDSUMMER NIGHT'S DREAM

THE CHARACTERS IN THE PLAY

THESEUS, Duke of Athens
HIPPOLYTA, Queen of the Amazons, betrothed to
    Theseus
EGEUS, Hermia's father
HERMIA, Egeus's daughter, in love with Lysander
LYSANDER, loved by Hermia
DEMETRIUS, suitor of Hermia
HELENA, in love with Demetrius
PHILOSTRATE, Theseus's Master of the Revels

OBERON, King of the Fairies
TITANIA, Queen of the Fairies
PUCK, or Robin Goodfellow
PEASEBLOSSOM ⎫
COBWEB   ⎪
MOTH   ⎬ Fairies
MUSTARDSEED ⎭

PETER QUINCE, a carpenter; Prologue in the interlude
NICK BOTTOM, a weaver; Pyramus in the interlude
FRANCIS FLUTE, a bellows-mender; Thisbe in the inter-
    lude
TOM SNOUT, a tinker; Wall in the interlude
SNUG, a joiner; Lion in the interlude
ROBIN STARVELING, a tailor; Moonshine in the interlude

Other fairies attending on Oberon and Titania
Lords and Attendants to Theseus and Hippolyta

Enter Theseus, Hippolyta, Philostrate,
and Attendants

THESEUS

Now, fair Hippolyta, our nuptial hour
Draws on apace. Four happy days bring in
Another moon – but O, methinks how slow
This old moon wanes! She lingers my desires,
Like to a stepdame or a dowager
Long withering out a young man's revenue.

HIPPOLYTA

Four days will quickly steep themselves in night;
Four nights will quickly dream away the time:
And then the moon – like to a silver bow
New-bent in heaven – shall behold the night   10
Of our solemnities.

THESEUS   Go, Philostrate,
Stir up the Athenian youth to merriments.
Awake the pert and nimble spirit of mirth.
Turn melancholy forth to funerals:
The pale companion is not for our pomp.   *Exit Philostrate*
Hippolyta, I wooed thee with my sword,
And won thy love doing thee injuries;
But I will wed thee in another key:
With pomp, with triumph, and with revelling.
        Enter Egeus and his daughter Hermia, and Lysander,
        and Demetrius

EGEUS

Happy be Theseus, our renownèd Duke.   20

THESEUS

Thanks, good Egeus. What's the news with thee?

EGEUS

Full of vexation come I, with complaint
Against my child, my daughter Hermia.
Stand forth, Demetrius! My noble lord,
This man hath my consent to marry her.
Stand forth, Lysander! – And, my gracious Duke,
This man hath bewitched the bosom of my child.
Thou, thou, Lysander, thou hast given her rhymes,
And interchanged love-tokens with my child.
30 Thou hast by moonlight at her window sung
With feigning voice verses of feigning love,
And stolen the impression of her fantasy.
With bracelets of thy hair, rings, gauds, conceits,
Knacks, trifles, nosegays, sweetmeats – messengers
Of strong prevailment in unhardened youth –
With cunning hast thou filched my daughter's heart,
Turned her obedience which is due to me
To stubborn harshness. And, my gracious Duke,
Be it so she will not here before your grace
40 Consent to marry with Demetrius,
I beg the ancient privilege of Athens:
As she is mine, I may dispose of her;
Which shall be either to this gentleman
Or to her death, according to our law
Immediately provided in that case.

THESEUS

What say you, Hermia? Be advised, fair maid:
To you your father should be as a god;
One that composed your beauties – yea, and one
To whom you are but as a form in wax
50 By him imprinted, and within his power
To leave the figure or disfigure it.

46

Demetrius is a worthy gentleman.

HERMIA

So is Lysander.

THESEUS   In himself he is;
But in this kind, wanting your father's voice,
The other must be held the worthier.

HERMIA

I would my father looked but with my eyes.

THESEUS

Rather your eyes must with his judgement look.

HERMIA

I do entreat your grace to pardon me.
I know not by what power I am made bold,
Nor how it may concern my modesty   60
In such a presence here to plead my thoughts;
But I beseech your grace that I may know
The worst that may befall me in this case
If I refuse to wed Demetrius.

THESEUS

Either to die the death, or to abjure
For ever the society of men.
Therefore, fair Hermia, question your desires,
Know of your youth, examine well your blood,
Whether, if you yield not to your father's choice,
You can endure the livery of a nun,   70
For aye to be in shady cloister mewed,
To live a barren sister all your life,
Chanting faint hymns to the cold fruitless moon.
Thrice blessèd they that master so their blood
To undergo such maiden pilgrimage;
But earthlier happy is the rose distilled
Than that which, withering on the virgin thorn,
Grows, lives, and dies in single blessedness.

HERMIA

So will I grow, so live, so die, my lord,
80 Ere I will yield my virgin patent up
Unto his lordship whose unwishèd yoke
My soul consents not to give sovereignty.

THESEUS

Take time to pause, and by the next new moon –
The sealing day betwixt my love and me
For everlasting bond of fellowship –
Upon that day either prepare to die
For disobedience to your father's will,
Or else to wed Demetrius, as he would,
Or on Diana's altar to protest
90 For aye austerity and single life.

DEMETRIUS

Relent, sweet Hermia; and, Lysander, yield
Thy crazèd title to my certain right.

LYSANDER

You have her father's love, Demetrius –
Let me have Hermia's. Do you marry him.

EGEUS

Scornful Lysander – true, he hath my love;
And what is mine my love shall render him;
And she is mine, and all my right of her
I do estate unto Demetrius.

LYSANDER

I am, my lord, as well derived as he,
100 As well possessed. My love is more than his,
My fortunes every way as fairly ranked –
If not with vantage – as Demetrius'.
And – which is more than all these boasts can be –
I am beloved of beauteous Hermia.
Why should not I then prosecute my right?
Demetrius – I'll avouch it to his head –

Made love to Nedar's daughter, Helena,
And won her soul; and she, sweet lady, dotes,
Devoutly dotes, dotes in idolatry
Upon this spotted and inconstant man.   110

THESEUS
I must confess that I have heard so much,
And with Demetrius thought to have spoke thereof;
But, being overfull of self affairs,
My mind did lose it. But Demetrius, come;
And come, Egeus. You shall go with me.
I have some private schooling for you both.
For you, fair Hermia, look you arm yourself
To fit your fancies to your father's will;
Or else the law of Athens yields you up –
Which by no means we may extenuate –   120
To death or to a vow of single life.
Come, my Hippolyta. What cheer, my love?
Demetrius and Egeus, go along;
I must employ you in some business
Against our nuptial, and confer with you
Of something nearly that concerns yourselves.

EGEUS
With duty and desire we follow you.
Exeunt all but Lysander and Hermia

LYSANDER
How now, my love? Why is your cheek so pale?
How chance the roses there do fade so fast?

HERMIA
Belike for want of rain, which I could well   130
Beteem them from the tempest of my eyes.

LYSANDER
Ay me! For aught that I could ever read,
Could ever hear by tale or history,
The course of true love never did run smooth;

But either it was different in blood –

HERMIA

O cross! – too high to be enthralled to low.

LYSANDER

Or else misgraffèd in respect of years –

HERMIA

O spite! – too old to be engaged to young.

LYSANDER

Or else it stood upon the choice of friends –

HERMIA

140 O hell! – to choose love by another's eyes.

LYSANDER

Or if there were a sympathy in choice,
War, death, or sickness did lay siege to it,
Making it momentany as a sound,
Swift as a shadow, short as any dream,
Brief as the lightning in the collied night,
That in a spleen unfolds both heaven and earth,
And – ere a man hath power to say 'Behold!' –
The jaws of darkness do devour it up.
So quick bright things come to confusion.

HERMIA

150 If then true lovers have been ever crossed
It stands as an edict in destiny.
Then let us teach our trial patience,
Because it is a customary cross,
As due to love as thoughts, and dreams, and sighs,
Wishes, and tears – poor fancy's followers.

LYSANDER

A good persuasion. Therefore hear me, Hermia:
I have a widow aunt, a dowager,
Of great revenue; and she hath no child.
From Athens is her house remote seven leagues;
160 And she respects me as her only son.

There, gentle Hermia, may I marry thee;
And to that place the sharp Athenian law
Cannot pursue us. If thou lovest me, then
Steal forth thy father's house tomorrow night,
And in the wood, a league without the town –
Where I did meet thee once with Helena
To do observance to a morn of May –
There will I stay for thee.

HERMIA   My good Lysander,
I swear to thee by Cupid's strongest bow,
By his best arrow with the golden head,   170
By the simplicity of Venus' doves,
By that which knitteth souls and prospers loves,
And by that fire which burned the Carthage queen
When the false Trojan under sail was seen,
By all the vows that ever men have broke –
In number more than ever women spoke,–
In that same place thou hast appointed me
Tomorrow truly will I meet with thee.

LYSANDER
Keep promise, love. Look – here comes Helena.
     Enter Helena

HERMIA
God speed, fair Helena! Whither away?   180

HELENA
Call you me fair? That 'fair' again unsay.
Demetrius loves your fair. O happy fair!
Your eyes are lodestars, and your tongue's sweet air
More tuneable than lark to shepherd's ear
When wheat is green, when hawthorn buds appear.
Sickness is catching. O, were favour so,
Yours would I catch, fair Hermia, ere I go.
My ear should catch your voice, my eye your eye,
My tongue should catch your tongue's sweet melody.

190 Were the world mine, Demetrius being bated,
The rest I'd give to be to you translated.
O, teach me how you look, and with what art
You sway the motion of Demetrius' heart.

HERMIA

I frown upon him, yet he loves me still.

HELENA

O that your frowns would teach my smiles such skill!

HERMIA

I give him curses, yet he gives me love.

HELENA

O that my prayers could such affection move!

HERMIA

The more I hate, the more he follows me.

HELENA

The more I love, the more he hateth me.

HERMIA

200 His folly, Helena, is no fault of mine.

HELENA

None but your beauty. Would that fault were mine!

HERMIA

Take comfort. He no more shall see my face.
Lysander and myself will fly this place.
Before the time I did Lysander see
Seemed Athens as a paradise to me.
O then, what graces in my love do dwell
That he hath turned a heaven unto a hell?

LYSANDER

Helen, to you our minds we will unfold.
Tomorrow night, when Phoebe doth behold
210 Her silver visage in the watery glass,
Decking with liquid pearl the bladed grass –
A time that lovers' flights doth still conceal –
Through Athens gates have we devised to steal.

HERMIA

And in the wood, where often you and I
Upon faint primrose beds were wont to lie,
Emptying our bosoms of their counsel sweet,
There my Lysander and myself shall meet,
And thence from Athens turn away our eyes
To seek new friends and stranger companies.
Farewell, sweet playfellow. Pray thou for us;   220
And good luck grant thee thy Demetrius.
Keep word, Lysander. We must starve our sight
From lovers' food till morrow deep midnight.

LYSANDER

I will, my Hermia.   *Exit Hermia*
          Helena, adieu!
As you on him, Demetrius dote on you. *Exit Lysander*

HELENA

How happy some o'er other some can be!
Through Athens I am thought as fair as she.
But what of that? Demetrius thinks not so;
He will not know what all but he do know.
And as he errs, doting on Hermia's eyes,   230
So I, admiring of his qualities.
Things base and vile, holding no quantity,
Love can transpose to form and dignity.
Love looks not with the eyes, but with the mind,
And therefore is winged Cupid painted blind.
Nor hath love's mind of any judgement taste;
Wings and no eyes figure unheedy haste.
And therefore is love said to be a child
Because in choice he is so oft beguiled.
As waggish boys in game themselves forswear,   240
So the boy love is perjured everywhere;
For ere Demetrius looked on Hermia's eyne
He hailed down oaths that he was only mine,

And when this hail some heat from Hermia felt,
So he dissolved, and showers of oaths did melt.
I will go tell him of fair Hermia's flight.
Then to the wood will he tomorrow night
Pursue her; and for this intelligence
If I have thanks it is a dear expense.
250 But herein mean I to enrich my pain,
To have his sight thither, and back again.   *Exit*

I.2   *Enter Quince the carpenter, and Snug the joiner, and*
               Bottom the weaver, and Flute the bellows-mender,
               and Snout the tinker, and Starveling the tailor

QUINCE Is all our company here?

BOTTOM You were best to call them generally, man by
    man, according to the scrip.

QUINCE Here is the scroll of every man's name which is
    thought fit through all Athens to play in our interlude
    before the Duke and the Duchess on his wedding day at
    night.

BOTTOM First, good Peter Quince, say what the play treats
    on; then read the names of the actors; and so grow to a
10 point.

QUINCE Marry, our play is *The most lamentable comedy*
    and most cruel death of Pyramus and Thisbe.

BOTTOM A very good piece of work, I assure you, and a
    merry. Now, good Peter Quince, call forth your actors
    by the scroll. Masters, spread yourselves.

QUINCE Answer as I call you. Nick Bottom, the weaver?

BOTTOM Ready! – Name what part I am for, and pro-
    ceed.

QUINCE You, Nick Bottom, are set down for Pyramus.

20 BOTTOM What is Pyramus? – a lover or a tyrant?

QUINCE A lover that kills himself, most gallant, for love.

54

BOTTOM That will ask some tears in the true performing of it. If I do it, let the audience look to their eyes! I will move storms. I will condole, in some measure. To the rest. – Yet my chief humour is for a tyrant. I could play Ercles rarely, or a part to tear a cat in, to make all split:

> The raging rocks
> And shivering shocks
> Shall break the locks
> Of prison gates,
> And Phibbus' car
> Shall shine from far
> And make and mar
> The foolish Fates.

30

This was lofty! – Now name the rest of the players. – This is Ercles' vein, a tyrant's vein. A lover is more condoling.

QUINCE Francis Flute, the bellows-mender?

FLUTE Here, Peter Quince.

QUINCE Flute, you must take Thisbe on you. 40

FLUTE What is Thisbe? – a wandering knight?

QUINCE It is the lady that Pyramus must love.

FLUTE Nay, faith, let not me play a woman – I have a beard coming.

QUINCE That's all one: you shall play it in a mask, and you may speak as small as you will.

BOTTOM An I may hide my face, let me play Thisbe too. I'll speak in a monstrous little voice: 'Thisne, Thisne!' 'Ah, Pyramus, my lover dear; thy Thisbe dear, and lady dear.' 50

QUINCE No, no; you must play Pyramus; and Flute, you Thisbe.

BOTTOM Well, proceed.

QUINCE Robin Starveling, the tailor?

STARVELING Here, Peter Quince.

QUINCE Robin Starveling, you must play Thisbe's
mother. Tom Snout, the tinker?

SNOUT Here, Peter Quince.

QUINCE You, Pyramus' father; myself, Thisbe's father;
60 Snug, the joiner, you the lion's part; and I hope here is
a play fitted.

SNUG Have you the lion's part written? Pray you, if it be,
give it me; for I am slow of study.

QUINCE You may do it extempore; for it is nothing but
roaring.

BOTTOM Let me play the lion too. I will roar that I will
do any man's heart good to hear me. I will roar that I
will make the Duke say 'Let him roar again; let him
roar again!'

70 QUINCE An you should do it too terribly you would fright
the Duchess and the ladies that they would shriek; and
that were enough to hang us all.

ALL That would hang us, every mother's son.

BOTTOM I grant you, friends, if you should fright the
ladies out of their wits they would have no more discretion but to hang us. But I will aggravate my voice so
that I will roar you as gently as any sucking dove. I will
roar you an 'twere any nightingale.

QUINCE You can play no part but Pyramus; for Pyramus
80 is a sweet-faced man; a proper man as one shall see in a
summer's day; a most lovely, gentlemanlike man. Therefore you must needs play Pyramus.

BOTTOM Well, I will undertake it. What beard were I
best to play it in?

QUINCE Why, what you will.

BOTTOM I will discharge it in either your straw-colour
beard, your orange-tawny beard, your purple-in-grain
beard, or your French-crown-colour beard, your perfect
yellow.

QUINCE Some of your French crowns have no hair at all; 90
and then you will play bare-faced! But, masters, here
are your parts, and I am to entreat you, request you, and
desire you to con them by tomorrow night, and meet me
in the palace wood a mile without the town by moonlight. There will we rehearse; for if we meet in the city
we shall be dogged with company, and our devices
known. In the meantime I will draw a bill of properties
such as our play wants. I pray you, fail me not.

BOTTOM We will meet, and there we may rehearse most
obscenely and courageously. Take pains, be perfect. 100
Adieu!

QUINCE At the Duke's oak we meet.

BOTTOM Enough; hold, or cut bowstrings.

Exeunt Bottom and his fellows

❋

Enter a Fairy at one door, and Puck (Robin Good- II.1
fellow) at another

PUCK

How now, spirit; whither wander you?

FAIRY

Over hill, over dale,
Thorough bush, thorough briar,
Over park, over pale,
Thorough flood, thorough fire –
I do wander everywhere
Swifter than the moon's sphere,
And I serve the Fairy Queen,
To dew her orbs upon the green.
The cowslips tall her pensioners be;   10
In their gold coats spots you see –

Those be rubies, fairy favours;
In those freckles live their savours.
I must go seek some dewdrops here,
And hang a pearl in every cowslip's ear.
Farewell, thou lob of spirits; I'll be gone.
Our Queen and all her elves come here anon.

PUCK

The King doth keep his revels here tonight.
Take heed the Queen come not within his sight,
20 For Oberon is passing fell and wrath
Because that she as her attendant hath
A lovely boy stolen from an Indian king.
She never had so sweet a changeling,
And jealous Oberon would have the child
Knight of his train, to trace the forests wild.
But she perforce withholds the lovèd boy,
Crowns him with flowers, and makes him all her joy.
And now they never meet – in grove or green,
By fountain clear or spangled starlight sheen –
30 But they do square, that all their elves for fear
Creep into acorn cups and hide them there.

FAIRY

Either I mistake your shape and making quite,
Or else you are that shrewd and knavish sprite
Called Robin Goodfellow. Are not you he
That frights the maidens of the villagery,
Skim milk, and sometimes labour in the quern,
And bootless make the breathless housewife churn,
And sometime make the drink to bear no barm,
Mislead night-wanderers, laughing at their harm?
40 Those that 'Hobgoblin' call you, and 'Sweet Puck',
You do their work, and they shall have good luck.
Are not you he?

PUCK   Thou speakest aright:

58

I am that merry wanderer of the night.
I jest to Oberon, and make him smile
When I a fat and bean-fed horse beguile,
Neighing in likeness of a filly foal;
And sometime lurk I in a gossip's bowl
In very likeness of a roasted crab;
And when she drinks, against her lips I bob,
And on her withered dewlap pour the ale.   50
The wisest aunt telling the saddest tale
Sometime for threefoot stool mistaketh me;
Then slip I from her bum. Down topples she,
And 'Tailor' cries, and falls into a cough;
And then the whole choir hold their hips and laugh,
And waxen in their mirth, and neeze, and swear
A merrier hour was never wasted there.
But room, Fairy: here comes Oberon.

FAIRY

And here my mistress. Would that he were gone!
    Enter Oberon, the King of Fairies, at one door, with
    his train; and Titania, the Queen, at another with hers

OBERON

Ill met by moonlight, proud Titania!   60

TITANIA

What, jealous Oberon? Fairy, skip hence.
I have forsworn his bed and company.

OBERON

Tarry, rash wanton! Am not I thy lord?

TITANIA

Then I must be thy lady. But I know
When thou hast stolen away from Fairyland
And in the shape of Corin sat all day
Playing on pipes of corn, and versing love
To amorous Phillida. Why art thou here
Come from the farthest step of India

70 But that, forsooth, the bouncing Amazon,
Your buskined mistress and your warrior love,
To Theseus must be wedded? – and you come
To give their bed ioy and prosperity.

OBERON

How canst thou thus, for shame, Titania,
Glance at my credit with Hippolyta,
Knowing I know thy love to Theseus?
Didst thou not lead him through the glimmering night
From Perigenia, whom he ravishèd,
And make him with fair Aegles break his faith,
80 With Ariadne, and Antiopa?

TITANIA

These are the forgeries of jealousy;
And never since the middle summer's spring
Met we on hill, in dale, forest, or mead,
By pavèd fountain or by rushy brook,
Or in the beachèd margent of the sea
To dance our ringlets to the whistling wind,
But with thy brawls thou hast disturbed our sport.
Therefore the winds, piping to us in vain,
As in revenge have sucked up from the sea
90 Contagious fogs which, falling in the land,
Hath every pelting river made so proud
That they have overborne their continents.
The ox hath therefore stretched his yoke in vain,
The ploughman lost his sweat, and the green corn
Hath rotted ere his youth attained a beard.
The fold stands empty in the drownèd field,
And crows are fatted with the murrion flock.
The nine men's morris is filled up with mud,
And the quaint mazes in the wanton green
100 For lack of tread are undistinguishable.
The human mortals want their winter cheer.

No night is now with hymn or carol blessed.
Therefore the moon, the governess of floods,
Pale in her anger, washes all the air,
That rheumatic diseases do abound;
And thorough this distemperature we see
The seasons alter; hoary-headed frosts
Fall in the fresh lap of the crimson rose,
And on old Hiems' thin and icy crown
An odorous chaplet of sweet summer buds   110
Is as in mockery set. The spring, the summer,
The childing autumn, angry winter change
Their wonted liveries, and the mazèd world
By their increase now knows not which is which.
And this same progeny of evils
Comes from our debate, from our dissension.
We are their parents and original.

OBERON
Do you amend it, then! It lies in you.
Why should Titania cross her Oberon?
I do but beg a little changeling boy   120
To be my henchman.
TITANIA   Set your heart at rest.
The fairy land buys not the child of me.
His mother was a votaress of my order,
And in the spicèd Indian air by night
Full often hath she gossiped by my side,
And sat with me on Neptune's yellow sands
Marking th'embarkèd traders on the flood,
When we have laughed to see the sails conceive
And grow big-bellied with the wanton wind;
Which she with pretty and with swimming gait   130
Following – her womb then rich with my young squire–
Would imitate, and sail upon the land
To fetch me trifles, and return again

As from a voyage, rich with merchandise.
But she, being mortal, of that boy did die,
And for her sake do I rear up her boy;
And for her sake I will not part with him.

OBERON

How long within this wood intend you stay?

TITANIA

Perchance till after Theseus' wedding day.
140 If you will patiently dance in our round
And see our moonlight revels, go with us.
If not, shun me, and I will spare your haunts.

OBERON

Give me that boy and I will go with thee.

TITANIA

Not for thy fairy kingdom! Fairies, away.
We shall chide downright if I longer stay.

Exit Titania with her train

OBERON

Well, go thy way. Thou shalt not from this grove
Till I torment thee for this injury.
My gentle Puck, come hither. Thou rememberest
Since once I sat upon a promontory
150 And heard a mermaid on a dolphin's back
Uttering such dulcet and harmonious breath
That the rude sea grew civil at her song,
And certain stars shot madly from their spheres
To hear the sea-maid's music?

PUCK   I remember.

OBERON

That very time I saw – but thou couldst not –
Flying between the cold moon and the earth
Cupid all armed. A certain aim he took
At a fair vestal thronèd by the west,
And loosed his loveshaft smartly from his bow

As it should pierce a hundred thousand hearts;   160
But I might see young Cupid's fiery shaft
Quenched in the chaste beams of the watery moon,
And the imperial votaress passed on
In maiden meditation, fancy-free.
Yet marked I where the bolt of Cupid fell:
It fell upon a little western flower,
Before, milk-white; now purple with love's wound:
And maidens call it 'love in idleness'.
Fetch me that flower – the herb I showed thee once.
The juice of it on sleeping eyelids laid   170
Will make or man or woman madly dote
Upon the next live creature that it sees.
Fetch me this herb, and be thou here again
Ere the leviathan can swim a league.

PUCK

I'll put a girdle round about the earth
In forty minutes!   *Exit*

OBERON   Having once this juice
I'll watch Titania when she is asleep,
And drop the liquor of it in her eyes.
The next thing then she, waking, looks upon –
Be it on lion, bear, or wolf, or bull,   180
On meddling monkey or on busy ape –
She shall pursue it with the soul of love.
And ere I take this charm from off her sight –
As I can take it with another herb –
I'll make her render up her page to me.
But who comes here? I am invisible,
And I will overhear their conference.
     Enter Demetrius, Helena following him

DEMETRIUS

I love thee not, therefore pursue me not.
Where is Lysander, and fair Hermia?

190 The one I'll slay; the other slayeth me.
Thou toldest me they were stolen unto this wood,
And here am I, and wood within this wood
Because I cannot meet my Hermia.
Hence, get thee gone, and follow me no more!

HELENA
You draw me, you hard-hearted adamant!
But yet you draw not iron: for my heart
Is true as steel. Leave you your power to draw,
And I shall have no power to follow you.

DEMETRIUS
Do I entice you? Do I speak you fair?
200 Or rather do I not in plainest truth
Tell you I do not nor I cannot love you?

HELENA
And even for that do I love you the more.
I am your spaniel; and, Demetrius,
The more you beat me I will fawn on you.
Use me but as your spaniel: spurn me, strike me,
Neglect me, lose me; only give me leave,
Unworthy as I am, to follow you.
What worser place can I beg in your love –
And yet a place of high respect with me –
210 Than to be usèd as you use your dog?

DEMETRIUS
Tempt not too much the hatred of my spirit;
For I am sick when I do look on thee.

HELENA
And I am sick when I look not on you.

DEMETRIUS
You do impeach your modesty too much,
To leave the city and commit yourself
Into the hands of one that loves you not;
To trust the opportunity of night

And the ill counsel of a desert place
With the rich worth of your virginity.

HELENA

Your virtue is my privilege. For that 220
It is not night when I do see your face,
Therefore I think I am not in the night;
Nor doth this wood lack worlds of company,
For you in my respect are all the world.
Then how can it be said I am alone
When all the world is here to look on me?

DEMETRIUS

I'll run from thee and hide me in the brakes,
And leave thee to the mercy of wild beasts.

HELENA

The wildest hath not such a heart as you.
Run when you will. The story shall be changed: 230
Apollo flies, and Daphne holds the chase;
The dove pursues the griffin; the mild hind
Makes speed to catch the tiger – bootless speed,
When cowardice pursues, and valour flies.

DEMETRIUS

I will not stay thy questions. Let me go;
Or if thou follow me, do not believe
But I shall do thee mischief in the wood.

HELENA

Ay – in the temple, in the town, the field,
You do me mischief. Fie, Demetrius,
Your wrongs do set a scandal on my sex. 240
We cannot fight for love, as men may do;
We should be wooed, and were not made to woo.

Exit Demetrius

I'll follow thee, and make a heaven of hell,
To die upon the hand I love so well.

Exit Helena

65

OBERON

Fare thee well, nymph. Ere he do leave this grove
Thou shalt fly him, and he shall seek thy love.
Enter Puck
Hast thou the flower there? Welcome, wanderer.

PUCK

Ay, there it is.

OBERON   I pray thee give it me.
I know a bank where the wild thyme blows,
250 Where oxlips and the nodding violet grows,
Quite overcanopied with luscious woodbine,
With sweet muskroses and with eglantine.
There sleeps Titania some time of the night,
Lulled in these flowers with dances and delight.
And there the snake throws her enamelled skin,
Weed wide enough to wrap a fairy in.
And with the juice of this I'll streak her eyes
And make her full of hateful fantasies.
Take thou some of it, and seek through this grove.
260 A sweet Athenian lady is in love
With a disdainful youth – anoint his eyes;
But do it when the next thing he espies
May be the lady. Thou shalt know the man
By the Athenian garments he hath on.
Effect it with some care, that he may prove
More fond on her than she upon her love.
And look thou meet me ere the first cock crow.

PUCK

Fear not, my lord; your servant shall do so.
Exeunt Oberon and Puck

TITANIA

   Come, now a roundel and a fairy song,
   Then for the third part of a minute hence:
   Some to kill cankers in the muskrose buds,
   Some war with reremice for their leathern wings
   To make my small elves coats, and some keep back
   The clamorous owl that nightly hoots and wonders
   At our quaint spirits. Sing me now asleep;
   Then to your offices, and let me rest.

     Fairies sing

FIRST FAIRY

     You spotted snakes with double tongue,
       Thorny hedgehogs, be not seen.   10
     Newts and blindworms, do no wrong,
       Come not near our Fairy Queen.

CHORUS

     Philomel with melody
     Sing in our sweet lullaby,
   Lulla, lulla, lullaby; lulla, lulla, lullaby.
       Never harm
       Nor spell nor charm
     Come our lovely lady nigh.
     So good night, with lullaby.

FIRST FAIRY

     Weaving spiders, come not here;   20
       Hence, you longlegged spinners, hence!
     Beetles black, approach not near,
       Worm nor snail, do no offence.

CHORUS

     Philomel with melody
     Sing in our sweet lullaby,
   Lulla, lulla, lullaby; lulla, lulla, lullaby.
       Never harm

Nor spell nor charm
Come our lovely lady nigh.
30   So good night, with lullaby.

Titania sleeps

SECOND FAIRY

Hence, away! Now all is well.
One aloof stand sentinel!

Exeunt Fairies

Enter Oberon
He squeezes the flower on Titania's eyes

OBERON

What thou seest when thou dost wake,
Do it for thy true love take;
Love and languish for his sake.
Be it ounce or cat or bear,
Pard, or boar with bristled hair
In thy eye that shall appear
When thou wakest, it is thy dear.
40   Wake when some vile thing is near!   *Exit*

Enter Lysander and Hermia

LYSANDER

Fair love, you faint with wandering in the wood;
   And – to speak truth – I have forgot our way.
We'll rest us, Hermia, if you think it good,
   And tarry for the comfort of the day.

HERMIA

Be it so, Lysander; find you out a bed,
For I upon this bank will rest my head.

LYSANDER

One turf shall serve as pillow for us both;
One heart, one bed, two bosoms, and one troth.

HERMIA

Nay, good Lysander, for my sake, my dear,
50   Lie further off yet; do not lie so near.

LYSANDER

O, take the sense, sweet, of my innocence!
Love takes the meaning in love's conference –
I mean that my heart unto yours is knit,
So that but one heart we can make of it.
Two bosoms interchainèd with an oath –
So then two bosoms and a single troth.
Then by your side no bed-room me deny,
For lying so, Hermia, I do not lie.

HERMIA

Lysander riddles very prettily.
Now much beshrew my manners and my pride   60
If Hermia meant to say Lysander lied.
But, gentle friend, for love and courtesy
Lie further off, in human modesty:
Such separation as may well be said
Becomes a virtuous bachelor and a maid,
So far be distant, and good night, sweet friend;
Thy love ne'er alter till thy sweet life end.

LYSANDER

Amen, amen, to that fair prayer say I,
And then end life when I end loyalty.
Here is my bed: sleep give thee all his rest.   70

HERMIA

With half that wish the wisher's eyes be pressed.
        They sleep
        Enter Puck

PUCK

Through the forest have I gone,
But Athenian found I none
On whose eyes I might approve
This flower's force in stirring love.
Night and silence. – Who is here?
Weeds of Athens he doth wear.

This is he my master said
Despisèd the Athenian maid;
80 And here the maiden, sleeping sound
On the dank and dirty ground.
Pretty soul, she durst not lie
Near this lack-love, this kill-courtesy.
Churl, upon thy eyes I throw
All the power this charm doth owe.

He squeezes the flower on Lysander's eyes

When thou wakest let love forbid
Sleep his seat on thy eyelid.
So, awake when I am gone;
For I must now to Oberon.　　　　　　　　*Exit*

Enter Demetrius and Helena, running

HELENA
90 Stay though thou kill me, sweet Demetrius!
DEMETRIUS
I charge thee hence; and do not haunt me thus.
HELENA
O, wilt thou darkling leave me? Do not so!
DEMETRIUS
Stay, on thy peril. I alone will go.　　　　*Exit*
HELENA
O, I am out of breath in this fond chase.
The more my prayer, the lesser is my grace.
Happy is Hermia, wheresoe'er she lies,
For she hath blessèd and attractive eyes.
How came her eyes so bright? Not with salt tears –
If so, my eyes are oftener washed than hers.
100 No, no – I am as ugly as a bear;
For beasts that meet me run away for fear.
Therefore no marvel though Demetrius
Do as a monster fly my presence thus.
What wicked and dissembling glass of mine

70

Made me compare with Hermia's sphery eyne?
But who is here? – Lysander on the ground?
Dead – or asleep? I see no blood, no wound.
Lysander, if you live, good sir, awake!

LYSANDER (*wakes*)
And run through fire I will for thy sweet sake!
Transparent Helena, nature shows art   110
That through thy bosom makes me see thy heart.
Where is Demetrius? O, how fit a word
Is that vile name to perish on my sword!

HELENA
Do not say so, Lysander, say not so.
What though he love your Hermia, lord, what though?
Yet Hermia still loves you. Then be content.

LYSANDER
Content with Hermia? No, I do repent
The tedious minutes I with her have spent.
Not Hermia but Helena I love.
Who will not change a raven for a dove?   120
The will of man is by his reason swayed,
And reason says you are the worthier maid.
Things growing are not ripe until their season;
So I, being young, till now ripe not to reason.
And touching now the point of human skill,
Reason becomes the marshal to my will,
And leads me to your eyes, where I o'erlook
Love's stories written in love's richest book.

HELENA
Wherefore was I to this keen mockery born?
When at your hands did I deserve this scorn?   130
Is't not enough, is't not enough young man
That I did never – no, nor never can –
Deserve a sweet look from Demetrius' eye
But you must flout my insufficiency?

Good troth, you do me wrong – good sooth, you do –
In such disdainful manner me to woo.
But fare you well. Perforce I must confess
I thought you lord of more true gentleness.
O, that a lady of one man refused

140   Should of another therefore be abused!   *Exit*

LYSANDER

She sees not Hermia. Hermia, sleep thou there,
And never mayst thou come Lysander near.
For, as a surfeit of the sweetest things
The deepest loathing to the stomach brings,
Or as the heresies that men do leave
Are hated most of those they did deceive,
So thou, my surfeit and my heresy,
Of all be hated, but the most of me!
And, all my powers, address your love and might

150   To honour Helen and to be her knight.   *Exit*

HERMIA (*wakes*)

Help me, Lysander, help me! Do thy best
To pluck this crawling serpent from my breast!
Ay me, for pity! – What a dream was here!
Lysander, look how I do quake with fear!
Methought a serpent ate my heart away,
And you sat smiling at his cruel prey.
Lysander – what, removed? Lysander, lord!
What, out of hearing? Gone? No sound, no word?
Alack, where are you? Speak an if you hear.

160   Speak, of all loves! I swoon almost with fear.
No? Then I well perceive you are not nigh.
Either death or you I'll find immediately.   *Exit*

*

Enter the clowns : Bottom, Quince, Snout, Starveling, III.1
Flute, and Snug

BOTTOM Are we all met?

QUINCE Pat, pat; and here's a marvellous convenient place
for our rehearsal. This green plot shall be our stage, this
hawthorn brake our tiring-house, and we will do it in
action as we will do it before the Duke.

BOTTOM Peter Quince!

QUINCE What sayest thou, Bully Bottom?

BOTTOM There are things in this comedy of Pyramus and
Thisbe that will never please. First, Pyramus must draw
a sword to kill himself, which the ladies cannot abide.   10
How answer you that?

SNOUT By 'r lakin, a parlous fear!

STARVELING I believe we must leave the killing out,
when all is done.

BOTTOM Not a whit. I have a device to make all well.
Write me a prologue, and let the prologue seem to say
we will do no harm with our swords, and that Pyramus
is not killed indeed; and for the more better assurance,
tell them that I, Pyramus, am not Pyramus, but Bottom
the weaver. This will put them out of fear.   20

QUINCE Well, we will have such a prologue; and it shall
be written in eight and six.

BOTTOM No, make it two more: let it be written in eight
and eight.

SNOUT Will not the ladies be afeard of the lion?

STARVELING I fear it, I promise you.

BOTTOM Masters, you ought to consider with yourself, to
bring in – God shield us – a lion among ladies is a most
dreadful thing; for there is not a more fearful wildfowl
than your lion living; and we ought to look to't.   30

SNOUT Therefore another prologue must tell he is not a
lion.

73

BOTTOM Nay, you must name his name, and half his face must be seen through the lion's neck, and he himself must speak through, saying thus, or to the same defect: 'Ladies', or 'Fair ladies – I would wish you', or 'I would request you', or 'I would entreat you – not to fear, not to tremble. My life for yours: if you think I come hither as a lion, it were pity of my life. No. I am no such

40 thing. I am a man, as other men are' – and there indeed let him name his name, and tell them plainly he is Snug the joiner.

QUINCE Well, it shall be so. But there is two hard things: that is, to bring the moonlight into a chamber – for, you know, Pyramus and Thisbe meet by moonlight.

SNUG Doth the moon shine that night we play our play?

BOTTOM A calendar, a calendar! Look in the almanac – find out moonshine, find out moonshine!

QUINCE Yes, it doth shine that night.

50 BOTTOM Why, then, may you leave a casement of the Great Chamber window – where we play – open, and the moon may shine in at the casement.

QUINCE Ay; or else one must come in with a bush of thorns and a lantern, and say he comes to disfigure or to present the person of Moonshine. Then there is another thing. We must have a wall in the Great Chamber; for Pyramus and Thisbe, says the story, did talk through the chink of a wall.

SNOUT You can never bring in a wall. What say you,

60 Bottom?

BOTTOM Some man or other must present Wall; and let him have some plaster, or some loam, or some roughcast about him to signify Wall; and let him hold his fingers thus, and through that cranny shall Pyramus and Thisbe whisper.

QUINCE If that may be, then all is well. Come, sit down

74

every mother's son, and rehearse your parts. Pyramus,
you begin. When you have spoken your speech, enter
into that brake; and so everyone according to his cue.

Enter Puck

PUCK

What hempen homespuns have we swaggering here   70
So near the cradle of the Fairy Queen?
What, a play toward? I'll be an auditor –
An actor too, perhaps, if I see cause.

QUINCE

Speak, Pyramus! Thisbe, stand forth!

BOTTOM *as Pyramus*

Thisbe, the flowers of odious savours sweet –

QUINCE Odours – odours!

BOTTOM *as Pyramus*

                ... odours savours sweet.
So hath thy breath, my dearest Thisbe dear.
But hark, a voice. Stay thou but here awhile,
And by and by I will to thee appear.   *Exit* 80

PUCK

A stranger Pyramus than e'er played here.   *Exit*

FLUTE Must I speak now?

QUINCE Ay, marry must you; for you must understand he
goes but to see a noise that he heard, and is to come
again.

FLUTE *as Thisbe*

Most radiant Pyramus, most lilywhite of hue,
    Of colour like the red rose on triumphant briar,
Most brisky juvenal, and eke most lovely Jew,
    As true as truest horse that yet would never tire,
I'll meet thee, Pyramus, at Ninny's tomb –   90

QUINCE 'Ninus' tomb', man! – Why, you must not speak
that yet. That you answer to Pyramus. You speak all

your part at once, cues and all. Pyramus, enter – your cue is past. It is 'never tire'.

FLUTE O!
    (*as Thisbe*)
As true as truest horse, that yet would never tire.
    Enter Puck, and Bottom with an ass's head

BOTTOM *as Pyramus*
If I were fair, fair Thisbe, I were only thine.

QUINCE O monstrous! O strange! We are haunted! Pray, masters! Fly, masters! Help!
    Exeunt Quince, Snug, Flute, Snout, and Starveling

PUCK
100   I'll follow you, I'll lead you about a round,
        Thorough bog, thorough bush, thorough brake, thorough briar,
    Sometime a horse I'll be, sometime a hound,
        A hog, a headless bear, sometime a fire,
    And neigh, and bark, and grunt and roar and burn
    Like horse, hound, hog, bear, fire at every turn.   *Exit*

BOTTOM Why do they run away? This is a knavery of them to make me afeard.
    Enter Snout

SNOUT O Bottom, thou art changed. What do I see on thee?

110 BOTTOM What do you see? You see an ass head of your own, do you?
                                                    Exit Snout
    Enter Quince

QUINCE Bless thee, Bottom! Bless thee! Thou art trans-lated!   *Exit*

BOTTOM I see their knavery! This is to make an ass of me, to fright me, if they could; but I will not stir from this place, do what they can. I will walk up and down here, and I will sing, that they shall hear I am not afraid.

(*sings*) The ousel cock so black of hue,
                     With orange-tawny bill,
              The throstle with his note so true,   120
                     The wren with little quill.

TITANIA (*wakes*)
   What angel wakes me from my flowery bed?

BOTTOM (*sings*)
                     The finch, the sparrow, and the lark,
                            The plainsong cuckoo grey,
                     Whose note full many a man doth mark
                            And dares not answer 'Nay'
   – for indeed, who would set his wit to so foolish a bird?
   Who would give a bird the lie, though he cry 'cuckoo'
   never so?

TITANIA
   I pray thee, gentle mortal, sing again!   130
   Mine ear is much enamoured of thy note.
   So is mine eye enthrallèd to thy shape,
   And thy fair virtue's force perforce doth move me
   On the first view to say, to swear, I love thee.

BOTTOM Methinks, mistress, you should have little reason
   for that. And yet, to say the truth, reason and love keep
   little company together nowadays – the more the pity
   that some honest neighbours will not make them friends.
   – Nay, I can gleek upon occasion.

TITANIA
   Thou art as wise as thou art beautiful.   140

BOTTOM Not so neither; but if I had wit enough to get
   out of this wood, I have enough to serve mine own turn.

TITANIA
   Out of this wood do not desire to go!
   Thou shalt remain here, whether thou wilt or no.
   I am a spirit of no common rate.
   The summer still doth tend upon my state,

And I do love thee. Therefore go with me.
I'll give thee fairies to attend on thee,
And they shall fetch thee jewels from the deep,
150 And sing while thou on pressèd flowers dost sleep;
And I will purge thy mortal grossness so
That thou shalt like an airy spirit go.
Peaseblossom, Cobweb, Moth, and Mustardseed!
  Enter the four Fairies
PEASEBLOSSOM Ready!
COBWEB And I!
MOTH And I!
MUSTARDSEED And I!
ALL Where shall we go?
TITANIA
Be kind and courteous to this gentleman.
160 Hop in his walks and gambol in his eyes;
Feed him with apricocks and dewberries,
With purple grapes, green figs, and mulberries.
The honey bags steal from the humble bees,
And for night-tapers crop their waxen thighs
And light them at the fiery glow-worms' eyes
To have my love to bed and to arise;
And pluck the wings from painted butterflies
To fan the moonbeams from his sleeping eyes.
Nod to him, elves, and do him courtesies.
170 PEASEBLOSSOM Hail, mortal!
COBWEB Hail!
MOTH Hail!
MUSTARDSEED Hail!
BOTTOM I cry your worships mercy, heartily. I beseech
  your worship's name.
COBWEB Cobweb.
BOTTOM I shall desire you of more acquaintance, good
  Master Cobweb – if I cut my finger I shall make bold

with you! – Your name, honest gentleman?

PEASEBLOSSOM Peaseblossom.   180

BOTTOM I pray you commend me to Mistress Squash,
your mother, and to Master Peascod, your father. Good
Master Peaseblossom, I shall desire you of more acquaintance, too. – Your name, I beseech you, sir?

MUSTARDSEED Mustardseed.

BOTTOM Good Master Mustardseed, I know your
patience well. That same cowardly, giantlike Oxbeef
hath devoured many a gentleman of your house. I
promise you, your kindred hath made my eyes water
ere now. I desire your more acquaintance, good Master   190
Mustardseed.

TITANIA
Come, wait upon him. Lead him to my bower.
    The moon methinks looks with a watery eye;
And when she weeps, weeps every little flower,
    Lamenting some enforcèd chastity.
    Tie up my lover's tongue; bring him silently.
                    Exit Titania with Bottom and the Fairies

I.2   *Enter Oberon, King of Fairies*

OBERON
I wonder if Titania be awaked;
Then what it was that next came in her eye,
Which she must dote on, in extremity.
Here comes my messenger.
          Enter Puck
                              How now, mad spirit?
What night-rule now about this haunted grove?

PUCK
My mistress with a monster is in love.
Near to her close and consecrated bower,
While she was in her dull and sleeping hour,

A crew of patches, rude mechanicals
10 That work for bread upon Athenian stalls,
Were met together to rehearse a play
Intended for great Theseus' nuptial day.
The shallowest thickskin of that barren sort,
Who Pyramus presented, in their sport
Forsook his scene and entered in a brake,
When I did him at this advantage take.
An ass's nole I fixèd on his head.
Anon his Thisbe must be answerèd,
And forth my mimic comes. When they him spy –
20 As wild geese that the creeping fowler eye,
Or russet-pated choughs, many in sort,
Rising and cawing at the gun's report,
Sever themselves and madly sweep the sky –
So at his sight away his fellows fly,
And at our stamp here o'er and o'er one falls.
He 'Murder!' cries, and help from Athens calls.
Their sense thus weak, lost with their fears thus strong,
Made senseless things begin to do them wrong.
For briars and thorns at their apparel snatch,
30 Some sleeves, some hats. From yielders all things catch.
I led them on in this distracted fear,
And left sweet Pyramus translated there;
When in that moment – so it came to pass –
Titania waked, and straightway loved an ass.

OBERON

This falls out better than I could devise!
But hast thou yet latched the Athenian's eyes
With the love juice, as I did bid thee do?

PUCK

I took him sleeping – that is finished too;
And the Athenian woman by his side,
40 That when he waked of force she must be eyed.

80

Enter Demetrius and Hermia

OBERON
Stand close. This is the same Athenian.

PUCK
This is the woman, but not this the man.

DEMETRIUS
O, why rebuke you him that loves you so?
Lay breath so bitter on your bitter foe.

HERMIA
Now I but chide; but I should use thee worse,
For thou, I fear, hast given me cause to curse.
If thou hast slain Lysander in his sleep,
Being o'er shoes in blood, plunge in the deep,
And kill me too.
The sun was not so true unto the day   50
As he to me. Would he have stolen away
From sleeping Hermia? I'll believe as soon
This whole earth may be bored, and that the moon
May through the centre creep, and so displease
Her brother's noontide with the Antipodes.
It cannot be but thou hast murdered him.
So should a murderer look; so dead, so grim.

DEMETRIUS
So should the murdered look, and so should I,
Pierced through the heart with your stern cruelty.
Yet you, the murderer, look as bright, as clear,   60
As yonder Venus in her glimmering sphere.

HERMIA
What's this to my Lysander? Where is he?
Ah, good Demetrius, wilt thou give him me?

DEMETRIUS
I had rather give his carcass to my hounds.

HERMIA
Out, dog! Out, cur! Thou drivest me past the bounds

Of maiden's patience. Hast thou slain him then?
Henceforth be never numbered among men.
O, once tell true – tell true, even for my sake.
Durst thou have looked upon him being awake?
70   And hast thou killed him sleeping? O, brave touch!
Could not a worm, an adder do so much?
An adder did it; for with doubler tongue
Than thine, thou serpent, never adder stung.

DEMETRIUS

You spend your passion on a misprised mood.
I am not guilty of Lysander's blood.
Nor is he dead, for aught that I can tell.

HERMIA

I pray thee, tell me then that he is well.

DEMETRIUS

An if I could, what should I get therefore?

HERMIA

A privilege never to see me more;
80   And from thy hated presence part I so.
See me no more, whether he be dead or no.   *Exit*

DEMETRIUS

There is no following her in this fierce vein.
Here therefore for a while I will remain.
So sorrow's heaviness doth heavier grow
For debt that bankrupt sleep doth sorrow owe,
Which now in some slight measure it will pay,
If for his tender here I make some stay.
    He lies down and sleeps

OBERON

What hast thou done? Thou hast mistaken quite,
And laid the love juice on some true love's sight.
90   Of thy misprision must perforce ensue
Some true love turned, and not a false turned true.

PUCK

    Then fate o'errules, that, one man holding truth,
    A million fail, confounding oath on oath.

OBERON

    About the wood go swifter than the wind,
    And Helena of Athens look thou find.
    All fancy-sick she is and pale of cheer
    With sighs of love, that costs the fresh blood dear.
    By some illusion see thou bring her here.
    I'll charm his eyes against she do appear.

PUCK

    I go, I go – look how I go –   100
    Swifter than arrow from the Tartar's bow.   *Exit*

OBERON

      Flower of this purple dye,
      Hit with Cupid's archery,
      Sink in apple of his eye.
        He squeezes the flower on Demetrius's eyes
      When his love he doth espy,
      Let her shine as gloriously
      As the Venus of the sky.
      When thou wakest, if she be by,
      Beg of her for remedy.
        Enter Puck

PUCK

      Captain of our fairy band,   110
      Helena is here at hand,
      And the youth mistook by me,
      Pleading for a lover's fee.
      Shall we their fond pageant see?
      Lord, what fools these mortals be!

OBERON

      Stand aside. The noise they make
      Will cause Demetrius to awake.

83

III.2

PUCK

> Then will two at once woo one –
> That must needs be sport alone;
> And those things do best please me
> That befall preposterously.
> *Enter Lysander and Helena*

LYSANDER

Why should you think that I should woo in scorn?
Scorn and derision never come in tears.
Look when I vow, I weep; and vows so born,
In their nativity all truth appears.
How can these things in me seem scorn to you,
Bearing the badge of faith to prove them true?

HELENA

You do advance your cunning more and more.
When truth kills truth, O devilish-holy fray!
These vows are Hermia's. Will you give her o'er?
Weigh oath with oath, and you will nothing weigh.
Your vows to her and me, put in two scales,
Will even weigh, and both as light as tales.

LYSANDER

I had no judgement when to her I swore.

HELENA

Nor none in my mind now you give her o'er.

LYSANDER

Demetrius loves her, and he loves not you.

DEMETRIUS (*wakes*)

O Helen, goddess, nymph, perfect, divine –
To what, my love, shall I compare thine eyne?
Crystal is muddy! O, how ripe in show
Thy lips – those kissing cherries – tempting grow!
That pure congealèd white, high Taurus' snow,
Fanned with the eastern wind, turns to a crow
When thou holdest up thy hand. O, let me kiss

This princess of pure white, this seal of bliss!

HELENA

O spite! O hell! I see you all are bent
To set against me for your merriment.
If you were civil and knew courtesy
You would not do me thus much injury.
Can you not hate me – as I know you do –
But you must join in souls to mock me too?   150
If you were men – as men you are in show –
You would not use a gentle lady so,
To vow, and swear, and superpraise my parts,
When, I am sure, you hate me with your hearts.
You both are rivals, and love Hermia;
And now both rivals to mock Helena.
A trim exploit, a manly enterprise –
To conjure tears up in a poor maid's eyes
With your derision. None of noble sort
Would so offend a virgin, and extort   160
A poor soul's patience, all to make you sport.

LYSANDER

You are unkind, Demetrius. Be not so,
For you love Hermia – this you know I know.
And hear: with all good will, with all my heart,
In Hermia's love I yield you up my part.
And yours of Helena to me bequeath,
Whom I do love, and will do to my death.

HELENA

Never did mockers waste more idle breath.

DEMETRIUS

Lysander, keep thy Hermia. I will none.
If e'er I loved her all that love is gone.   170
My heart to her but as guestwise sojourned,
And now to Helen is it home returned,
There to remain.

LYSANDER   Helen, it is not so.

DEMETRIUS

Disparage not the faith thou dost not know,
Lest to thy peril thou aby it dear.
Look where thy love comes: yonder is thy dear.
    Enter Hermia

HERMIA

Dark night that from the eye his function takes
The ear more quick of apprehension makes.
Wherein it doth impair the seeing sense
It pays the hearing double recompense.
Thou art not by mine eye, Lysander, found;
Mine ear – I thank it – brought me to thy sound.
But why unkindly didst thou leave me so?

LYSANDER

Why should he stay whom love doth press to go?

HERMIA

What love could press Lysander from my side?

LYSANDER

Lysander's love, that would not let him bide:
Fair Helena, who more engilds the night
Than all yon fiery oes and eyes of light,
Why seekest thou me? Could not this make thee know
The hate I bare thee made me leave thee so?

HERMIA

You speak not as you think. It cannot be.

HELENA

Lo, she is one of this confederacy.
Now I perceive they have conjoined all three
To fashion this false sport in spite of me.
Injurious Hermia, most ungrateful maid,
Have you conspired, have you with these contrived
To bait me with this foul derision?
Is all the counsel that we two have shared –

180

190

The sisters' vows, the hours that we have spent
When we have chid the hasty-footed time   200
For parting us – O, is all forgot?
All schooldays' friendship, childhood innocence?
We, Hermia, like two artificial gods
Have with our needles created both one flower,
Both on one sampler, sitting on one cushion,
Both warbling of one song, both in one key,
As if our hands, our sides, voices, and minds
Had been incorporate. So we grew together
Like to a double cherry, seeming parted
But yet an union in partition,   210
Two lovely berries moulded on one stem,
So with two seeming bodies but one heart,
Two of the first, like coats in heraldry,
Due but to one, and crownèd with one crest.
And will you rent our ancient love asunder,
To join with men in scorning your poor friend?
It is not friendly, 'tis not maidenly.
Our sex as well as I may chide you for it,
Though I alone do feel the injury.

HERMIA

I am amazèd at your passionate words.   220
I scorn you not; it seems that you scorn me.

HELENA

Have you not set Lysander, as in scorn,
To follow me and praise my eyes and face?
And made your other love, Demetrius –
Who even but now did spurn me with his foot –
To call me goddess, nymph, divine and rare,
Precious, celestial? Wherefore speaks he this
To her he hates? And wherefore doth Lysander
Deny your love, so rich within his soul,
And tender me forsooth affection,   230

But by your setting on, by your consent?
What though I be not so in grace as you,
So hung upon with love, so fortunate,
But miserable most, to love unloved:
This you should pity rather than despise.

HERMIA

I understand not what you mean by this.

HELENA

Ay, do! Persever, counterfeit sad looks,
Make mouths upon me when I turn my back,
Wink each at other, hold the sweet jest up.
240   This sport well carried shall be chroniclèd.
If you have any pity, grace, or manners,
You would not make me such an argument.
But fare ye well. 'Tis partly my own fault,
Which death or absence soon shall remedy.

LYSANDER

Stay, gentle Helena, hear my excuse,
My love, my life, my soul, fair Helena!

HELENA

O, excellent!

HERMIA (*to Lysander*)

          Sweet, do not scorn her so.

DEMETRIUS

If she cannot entreat, I can compel.

LYSANDER

Thou canst compel no more than she entreat.
250   Thy threats have no more strength than her weak
       prayers.
Helen, I love thee. By my life, I do.
I swear by that which I will lose for thee
To prove him false that says I love thee not.

DEMETRIUS

I say I love thee more than he can do.

LYSANDER

If thou say so, withdraw, and prove it too.

DEMETRIUS

Quick, come.

HERMIA   Lysander, whereto tends all this?

LYSANDER

Away, you Ethiope!

DEMETRIUS   No, no. He'll

Seem to break loose, take on as he would follow,

But yet come not. (*To Lysander*) You are a tame man, go.

LYSANDER

Hang off, thou cat, thou burr! Vile thing, let loose,   260

Or I will shake thee from me like a serpent.

HERMIA

Why are you grown so rude? What change is this,

Sweet love?

LYSANDER   Thy love? – out, tawny Tartar, out;

Out, loathèd medicine! O hated potion, hence!

HERMIA

Do you not jest?

HELENA   Yes, sooth, and so do you.

LYSANDER

Demetrius, I will keep my word with thee.

DEMETRIUS

I would I had your bond; for I perceive

A weak bond holds you. I'll not trust your word.

LYSANDER

What? Should I hurt her, strike her, kill her dead?

Although I hate her, I'll not harm her so.   270

HERMIA

What? Can you do me greater harm than hate?

Hate me? Wherefore? O me, what news, my love?

Am not I Hermia? Are not you Lysander?

I am as fair now as I was erewhile.

Since night you loved me; yet since night you left
   me.
Why then, you left me – O, the gods forbid! –
In earnest, shall I say?

LYSANDER   Ay, by my life;
And never did desire to see thee more.
Therefore be out of hope, of question, of doubt,
280   Be certain. Nothing truer – 'tis no jest
That I do hate thee and love Helena.

HERMIA

O me, you juggler, you canker-blossom,
You thief of love! What, have you come by night
And stolen my love's heart from him?

HELENA   Fine, i'faith.
Have you no modesty, no maiden shame,
No touch of bashfulness? What, will you tear
Impatient answers from my gentle tongue?
Fie, fie, you counterfeit, you puppet, you!

HERMIA

Puppet? Why so? – Ay, that way goes the game.
290   Now I perceive that she hath made compare
Between our statures. She hath urged her height,
And with her personage, her tall personage,
Her height, forsooth, she hath prevailed with him.
And are you grown so high in his esteem
Because I am so dwarfish and so low?
How low am I, thou painted maypole? Speak!
How low am I? – I am not yet so low
But that my nails can reach unto thine eyes.

HELENA

I pray you, though you mock me, gentlemen,
300   Let her not hurt me. I was never curst.
I have no gift at all in shrewishness.
I am a right maid for my cowardice!

Let her not strike me. You perhaps may think
Because she is something lower than myself
That I can match her. . . .

HERMIA   Lower? Hark, again!

HELENA

Good Hermia, do not be so bitter with me.
I evermore did love you, Hermia;
Did ever keep your counsels, never wronged you,
Save that in love unto Demetrius
I told him of your stealth unto this wood.   310
He followed you. For love I followed him.
But he hath chid me hence, and threatened me
To strike me, spurn me – nay, to kill me too.
And now, so you will let me quiet go,
To Athens will I bear my folly back
And follow you no further. Let me go.
You see how simple and how fond I am.

HERMIA

Why, get you gone! Who is't that hinders you?

HELENA

A foolish heart that I leave here behind.

HERMIA

What, with Lysander?

HELENA   With Demetrius.   320

LYSANDER

Be not afraid; she shall not harm thee, Helena.

DEMETRIUS

No, sir. She shall not, though you take her part.

HELENA

O, when she is angry she is keen and shrewd.
She was a vixen when she went to school,
And though she be but little, she is fierce.

HERMIA

Little again? Nothing but low and little?

91

Why will you suffer her to flout me thus?
Let me come to her.

LYSANDER   Get you gone, you dwarf,
You minimus of hindering knot-grass made,
You bead, you acorn.

330 DEMETRIUS   You are too officious
In her behalf that scorns your services.
Let her alone. Speak not of Helena,
Take not her part; for if thou dost intend
Never so little show of love to her,
Thou shalt aby it.

LYSANDER   Now she holds me not.
Now follow – if thou darest – to try whose right
Of thine or mine is most in Helena.

DEMETRIUS
Follow? Nay, I'll go with thee, cheek by jowl.
                    Exeunt Demetrius and Lysander

HERMIA
You, mistress – all this coil is 'long of you.
Nay – go not back.

340 HELENA   I will not trust you, I,
Nor longer stay in your curst company.
Your hands than mine are quicker for a fray.
My legs are longer, though, to run away!   *Exit*

HERMIA
I am amazed, and know not what to say!   *Exit*
          Oberon and Puck come forward

OBERON
This is thy negligence. Still thou mistakest,
Or else committest thy knaveries wilfully.

PUCK
Believe me, King of shadows, I mistook.
Did not you tell me I should know the man
By the Athenian garments he had on?

And so far blameless proves my enterprise 350
That I have 'nointed an Athenian's eyes.
And so far am I glad it so did sort,
As this their jangling I esteem a sport.

OBERON

Thou seest these lovers seek a place to fight.
Hie therefore, Robin, overcast the night.
The starry welkin cover thou anon
With drooping fog as black as Acheron,
And lead these testy rivals so astray
As one come not within another's way.
Like to Lysander sometime frame thy tongue, 360
Then stir Demetrius up with bitter wrong,
And sometime rail thou like Demetrius;
And from each other look thou lead them thus
Till o'er their brows death-counterfeiting sleep
With leaden legs and batty wings doth creep.
Then crush this herb into Lysander's eye –
Whose liquor hath this virtuous property,
To take from thence all error with his might,
And make his eyeballs roll with wonted sight.
When they next wake, all this derision 370
Shall seem a dream and fruitless vision,
And back to Athens shall the lovers wend
With league whose date till death shall never end.
Whiles I in this affair do thee employ
I'll to my Queen and beg her Indian boy,
And then I will her charmèd eye release
From monster's view, and all things shall be peace.

PUCK

My fairy lord, this must be done with haste,
For night's swift dragons cut the clouds full fast,
And yonder shines Aurora's harbinger, 380
At whose approach ghosts wandering here and there

Troop home to churchyards. Damnèd spirits all
That in crossways and floods have burial
Already to their wormy beds are gone.
For fear lest day should look their shames upon
They wilfully themselves exile from light,
And must for aye consort with black-browed night.

OBERON

But we are spirits of another sort.
I with the morning's love have oft made sport,
390 And like a forester the groves may tread
Even till the eastern gate all fiery red
Opening on Neptune with fair blessèd beams
Turns into yellow gold his salt green streams.
But notwithstanding, haste, make no delay;
We may effect this business yet ere day.   *Exit*

PUCK

Up and down, up and down,
I will lead them up and down.
I am feared in field and town.
Goblin, lead them up and down.
400 Here comes one.
        Enter Lysander

LYSANDER

Where art thou, proud Demetrius? Speak thou now.

PUCK (*in Demetrius's voice*)

Here, villain, drawn and ready! Where art thou?

LYSANDER

I will be with thee straight.

PUCK (*in Demetrius's voice*)   Follow me then
To plainer ground.   *Exit Lysander*
        Enter Demetrius

DEMETRIUS   Lysander, speak again.
Thou runaway, thou coward – art thou fled?
Speak. In some bush? Where dost thou hide thy head?

94

PUCK (*in Lysander's voice*)
  Thou coward, art thou bragging to the stars,
  Telling the bushes that thou lookest for wars,
  And wilt not come? Come, recreant. Come, thou child,
  I'll whip thee with a rod. He is defiled   410
  That draws a sword on thee.

DEMETRIUS   Yea, art thou there?

PUCK (*in Lysander's voice*)
  Follow my voice. We'll try no manhood here.

               Exeunt Puck and Demetrius

    Enter Lysander

LYSANDER
  He goes before me, and still dares me on;
  When I come where he calls, then he is gone.
  The villain is much lighter-heeled than I.
  I followed fast, but faster he did fly,
  That fallen am I in dark uneven way,
  And here will rest me. (*He lies down*) Come, thou gentle
     day,
  For if but once thou show me thy grey light
  I'll find Demetrius and revenge this spite.   420

    He sleeps
    Enter Puck and Demetrius

PUCK (*in Lysander's voice*)
  Ho, ho, ho, coward! Why comest thou not?

DEMETRIUS
  Abide me if thou darest, for well I wot
  Thou runnest before me, shifting every place,
  And darest not stand nor look me in the face.
  Where art thou now?

PUCK (*in Lysander's voice*)
               Come hither; I am here.

DEMETRIUS
  Nay, then thou mockest me. Thou shalt buy this dear

III.2

If ever I thy face by daylight see.
Now, go thy way. Faintness constraineth me
To measure out my length on this cold bed.
430 By day's approach look to be visited.
He lies down and sleeps
Enter Helena

HELENA

O weary night! O long and tedious night,
 Abate thy hours, shine comforts from the East,
That I may back to Athens by daylight
 From these that my poor company detest.
And sleep, that sometimes shuts up sorrow's eye,
Steal me awhile from mine own company.
She lies down and sleeps

PUCK

Yet but three? Come one more,
Two of both kinds makes up four.
Here she comes, curst and sad.
440 Cupid is a knavish lad
Thus to make poor females mad.
Enter Hermia

HERMIA

Never so weary, never so in woe,
 Bedabbled with the dew, and torn with briars –
I can no further crawl, no further go.
 My legs can keep no pace with my desires.
Here will I rest me till the break of day.
Heavens shield Lysander, if they mean a fray.
She lies down and sleeps

PUCK

On the ground
Sleep sound.
450 I'll apply
To your eye,

96

Gentle lover, remedy.

He squeezes the juice on Lysander's eyes
   When thou wakest,
   Thou takest
   True delight
   In the sight
Of thy former lady's eye.
And the country proverb known,
That every man should take his own,
In your waking shall be shown.   460
   Jack shall have Jill;
   Naught shall go ill.
The man shall have his mare again, and all shall be well.

             Exit

       ✻

Enter Titania, and Bottom, and Fairies; and Oberon IV.1
behind them

TITANIA
 Come, sit thee down upon this flowery bed
  While I thy amiable cheeks do coy,
 And stick muskroses in thy sleek, smooth head,
  And kiss thy fair large ears, my gentle joy.
BOTTOM Where's Peaseblossom?
PEASEBLOSSOM Ready.
BOTTOM Scratch my head, Peaseblossom. Where's
 Monsieur Cobweb?
COBWEB Ready.
BOTTOM Monsieur Cobweb, good Monsieur, get you your 10
 weapons in your hand and kill me a red-hipped humble
 bee on the top of a thistle; and, good Monsieur, bring
 me the honey bag. Do not fret yourself too much in the

action, Monsieur; and, good Monsieur, have a care the
honey bag break not, I would be loath to have you over-
flown with a honey bag, signor. Where's Monsieur
Mustardseed?

MUSTARDSEED Ready.

BOTTOM Give me your neaf, Monsieur Mustardseed.
20 Pray you, leave your courtesy, good Monsieur.

MUSTARDSEED What's your will?

BOTTOM Nothing, good Monsieur, but to help Cavalery
Cobweb to scratch. I must to the barber's, Monsieur,
for methinks I am marvellous hairy about the face. And
I am such a tender ass, if my hair do but tickle me, I
must scratch.

TITANIA
What, wilt thou hear some music, my sweet love?

BOTTOM I have a reasonable good ear in music. Let's have
the tongs and the bones.

TITANIA
30 Or say, sweet love, what thou desirest to eat.

BOTTOM Truly, a peck of provender. I could munch your
good dry oats. Methinks I have a great desire to a bottle
of hay. Good hay, sweet hay hath no fellow.

TITANIA
I have a venturous fairy that shall seek
The squirrel's hoard, and fetch thee new nuts.

BOTTOM I had rather have a handful or two of dried pease.
But, I pray you, let none of your people stir me. I have
an exposition of sleep come upon me.

TITANIA
Sleep thou, and I will wind thee in my arms.
40 Fairies be gone, and be all ways away.   *Exeunt Fairies*
So doth the woodbine the sweet honeysuckle
Gently entwist; the female ivy so
Enrings the barky fingers of the elm.

O, how I love thee! How I dote on thee!
>   *They sleep. Enter Puck*
OBERON (*comes forward*)
>   Welcome, good Robin. Seest thou this sweet sight?
>   Her dotage now I do begin to pity.
>   For, meeting her of late behind the wood
>   Seeking sweet favours for this hateful fool,
>   I did upbraid her and fall out with her,
>   For she his hairy temples then had rounded   50
>   With coronet of fresh and fragrant flowers.
>   And that same dew which sometime on the buds
>   Was wont to swell, like round and orient pearls,
>   Stood now within the pretty flowerets' eyes
>   Like tears that did their own disgrace bewail.
>   When I had at my pleasure taunted her,
>   And she in mild terms begged my patience,
>   I then did ask of her her changeling child,
>   Which straight she gave me, and her fairy sent
>   To bear him to my bower in Fairyland.   60
>   And now I have the boy I will undo
>   This hateful imperfection of her eyes.
>   And, gentle Puck, take this transformèd scalp
>   From off the head of this Athenian swain,
>   That, he awaking when the other do,
>   May all to Athens back again repair
>   And think no more of this night's accidents
>   But as the fierce vexation of a dream.
>   But first I will release the Fairy Queen.
>   (*o Titania*)
>   Be as thou wast wont to be;   70
>   See as thou wast wont to see.
>   Dian's bud o'er Cupid's flower
>   Hath such force and blessèd power.
Now, my Titania, wake you, my sweet Queen!

TITANIA (*wakes*)
My Oberon, what visions have I seen!
Methought I was enamoured of an ass.

OBERON
There lies your love.

TITANIA   How came these things to pass?
O, how mine eyes do loathe his visage now!

OBERON
Silence awhile! Robin, take off this head.
80   Titania, music call, and strike more dead
Than common sleep of all these five the sense.

TITANIA
Music, ho! Music such as charmeth sleep.

PUCK (*to Bottom, removing the ass's head*)
Now when thou wakest with thine own fool's eyes peep.

OBERON
Sound, music! (*Music*) Come, my Queen, take hands
        with me,
And rock the ground whereon these sleepers be.
        They dance
Now thou and I are new in amity,
And will tomorrow midnight solemnly
Dance in Duke Theseus' house triumphantly,
And bless it to all fair prosperity.
90   There shall the pairs of faithful lovers be
Wedded with Theseus all in jollity.

PUCK
        Fairy king, attend, and mark:
        I do hear the morning lark.

OBERON
        Then, my queen, in silence sad,
        Trip we after night's shade.
        We the globe can compass soon,
        Swifter than the wandering moon.

TITANIA

    Come, my lord, and in our flight
    Tell me how it came this night
    That I sleeping here was found   100
    With these mortals on the ground.

                Exeunt Oberon, Titania, and Puck
    Horns sound. Enter Theseus with Hippolyta, Egeus,
    and all his train

THESEUS

  Go, one of you; find out the forester;
  For now our observation is performed.
  And since we have the vaward of the day,
  My love shall hear the music of my hounds.
  Uncouple in the western valley; let them go.
  Dispatch, I say, and find the forester. *Exit an Attendant*
  We will, fair Queen, up to the mountain's top,
  And mark the musical confusion
  Of hounds and echo in conjunction.   110

HIPPOLYTA

  I was with Hercules and Cadmus once,
  When in a wood of Crete they bayed the bear
  With hounds of Sparta. Never did I hear
  Such gallant chiding, for besides the groves,
  The skies, the fountains, every region near
  Seemed all one mutual cry. I never heard
  So musical a discord, such sweet thunder.

THESEUS

  My hounds are bred out of the Spartan kind;
  So flewed, so sanded; and their heads are hung
  With ears that sweep away the morning dew;   120
  Crook-kneed; and dewlapped like Thessalian bulls;
  Slow in pursuit, but matched in mouth like bells,
  Each under each. A cry more tuneable
  Was never hallooed to nor cheered with horn

In Crete, in Sparta, nor in Thessaly.
Judge when you hear.
    He sees the sleepers
                   But soft, what nymphs are these?

EGEUS

My lord, this is my daughter here asleep,
And this Lysander; this Demetrius is,
This Helena – old Nedar's Helena.
130 I wonder of their being here together.

THESEUS

No doubt they rose up early to observe
The rite of May, and hearing our intent
Came here in grace of our solemnity.
But speak, Egeus: is not this the day
That Hermia should give answer of her choice?

EGEUS It is, my lord.

THESEUS

Go, bid the huntsmen wake them with their horns.
    Horns sound; the lovers wake; shout within; the
    lovers start up
Good morrow, friends – Saint Valentine is past!
Begin these woodbirds but to couple now?

LYSANDER

Pardon, my lord.
140 THESEUS   I pray you all, stand up.
I know you two are rival enemies.
How comes this gentle concord in the world,
That hatred is so far from jealousy
To sleep by hate, and fear no enmity?

LYSANDER

My lord, I shall reply amazedly,
Half sleep, half waking. But as yet, I swear,
I cannot truly say how I came here.
But as I think – for truly would I speak –

And now I do bethink me, so it is:
I came with Hermia hither. Our intent   150
Was to be gone from Athens where we might
Without the peril of the Athenian law . . .

EGEUS

Enough, enough – my lord, you have enough!
I beg the law, the law upon his head.
They would have stolen away, they would, Demetrius,
Thereby to have defeated you and me –
You of your wife, and me of my consent –
Of my consent that she should be your wife.

DEMETRIUS

My lord, fair Helen told me of their stealth,
Of this their purpose hither to this wood,   160
And I in fury hither followed them,
Fair Helena in fancy following me.
But, my good lord – I wot not by what power,
But by some power it is – my love to Hermia,
Melted as the snow, seems to me now
As the remembrance of an idle gaud
Which in my childhood I did dote upon;
And all the faith, the virtue of my heart,
The object and the pleasure of mine eye,
Is only Helena. To her, my lord,   170
Was I betrothed ere I saw Hermia;
But like a sickness did I loathe this food.
But, as in health come to my natural taste,
Now I do wish it, love it, long for it,
And will for evermore be true to it.

THESEUS

Fair lovers, you are fortunately met.
Of this discourse we more will hear anon.
Egeus, I will overbear your will;
For in the temple by and by with us

180   These couples shall eternally be knit.
    And – for the morning now is something worn –
    Our purposed hunting shall be set aside.
    Away with us to Athens. Three and three,
    We'll hold a feast in great solemnity.
    Come, Hippolyta.
          Exit Theseus with Hippolyta, Egeus, and his train

DEMETRIUS
    These things seem small and undistinguishable,
    Like far-off mountains turnèd into clouds.

HERMIA
    Methinks I see these things with parted eye,
    When everything seems double.

HELENA   So methinks,
190   And I have found Demetrius, like a jewel,
    Mine own and not mine own.

DEMETRIUS   Are you sure
    That we are awake? It seems to me
    That yet we sleep, we dream. Do not you think
    The Duke was here, and bid us follow him?

HERMIA
    Yea, and my father.

HELENA   And Hippolyta.

LYSANDER
    And he did bid us follow to the temple.

DEMETRIUS
    Why, then, we are awake. Let's follow him,
    And by the way let's recount our dreams.
          Exeunt Demetrius, Helena, Lysander, and Hermia
          Bottom wakes

BOTTOM When my cue comes, call me, and I will answer.
200   My next is 'Most fair Pyramus'. Heigh ho! Peter
    Quince! Flute the bellows-mender! Snout the tinker!
    Starveling! God's my life – stolen hence and left me

asleep! – I have had a most rare vision. I have had a dream past the wit of man to say what dream it was. Man is but an ass if he go about to expound this dream. Methought I was – there is no man can tell what. Methought I was – and methought I had – but man is but a patched fool if he will offer to say what methought I had. The eye of man hath not heard, the ear of man hath not seen, man's hand is not able to taste, his tongue to conceive, 210 nor his heart to report what my dream was! I will get Peter Quince to write a ballad of this dream. It shall be called 'Bottom's Dream', because it hath no bottom; and I will sing it in the latter end of a play before the Duke. Peradventure, to make it the more gracious, I shall sing it at her death.

Exit

Enter Quince, Flute, Snout, and Starveling IV.2

QUINCE Have you sent to Bottom's house? Is he come home yet?

STARVELING He cannot be heard of. Out of doubt he is transported.

FLUTE If he come not, then the play is marred. It goes not forward. Doth it?

QUINCE It is not possible. You have not a man in all Athens able to discharge Pyramus but he.

FLUTE No, he hath simply the best wit of any handicraft man in Athens. 10

QUINCE Yea, and the best person, too; and he is a very paramour for a sweet voice.

FLUTE You must say 'paragon'. A paramour is – God bless us – a thing of naught.

Enter Snug the joiner

SNUG Masters, the Duke is coming from the temple, and

there is two or three lords and ladies more married. If
our sport had gone forward, we had all been made men.

FLUTE O, sweet Bully Bottom! Thus hath he lost sixpence
a day during his life. He could not have scaped sixpence
20 a day. An the Duke had not given him sixpence a day for
playing Pyramus, I'll be hanged. He would have de-
served it. Sixpence a day in Pyramus, or nothing.

Enter Bottom

BOTTOM Where are these lads? Where are these hearts?

QUINCE Bottom! O most courageous day! O most happy
hour!

BOTTOM Masters, I am to discourse wonders – but ask
me not what; for if I tell you, I am not true Athenian. – I
will tell you everything, right as it fell out!

QUINCE Let us hear, sweet Bottom!

30 BOTTOM Not a word of me! All that I will tell you is – that
the Duke hath dined. Get your apparel together, good
strings to your beards, new ribbons to your pumps.
Meet presently at the palace. Every man look o'er his
part. For the short and the long is, our play is preferred.
In any case, let Thisbe have clean linen; and let not him
that plays the lion pare his nails, for they shall hang out
for the lion's claws. And, most dear actors, eat no onions
nor garlic; for we are to utter sweet breath, and I do
not doubt but to hear them say it is a sweet comedy. No
40 more words. Away – go, away!

Exeunt Bottom and his fellows

✳

HIPPOLYTA
'Tis strange, my Theseus, that these lovers speak of.

THESEUS
More strange than true. I never may believe
These antique fables, nor these fairy toys.
Lovers and madmen have such seething brains,
Such shaping fantasies, that apprehend
More than cool reason ever comprehends.
The lunatic, the lover, and the poet
Are of imagination all compact.
One sees more devils than vast hell can hold.
That is the madman. The lover, all as frantic,   10
Sees Helen's beauty in a brow of Egypt.
The poet's eye, in a fine frenzy rolling,
Doth glance from heaven to earth, from earth to heaven.
And as imagination bodies forth
The forms of things unknown, the poet's pen
Turns them to shapes, and gives to airy nothing
A local habitation and a name.
Such tricks hath strong imagination
That if it would but apprehend some joy,
It comprehends some bringer of that joy.   20
Or in the night, imagining some fear,
How easy is a bush supposed a bear?

HIPPOLYTA
But all the story of the night told over,
And all their minds transfigured so together,
More witnesseth than fancy's images,
And grows to something of great constancy;
But howsoever, strange and admirable.
    *Enter the lovers : Lysander, Demetrius, Hermia, and
    Helena*

THESEUS

Here come the lovers, full of joy and mirth.
Joy, gentle friends, joy and fresh days of love
Accompany your hearts.

30 LYSANDER　　　　　　　More than to us

Wait in your royal walks, your board, your bed.

THESEUS

Come now, what masques, what dances shall we have
To wear away this long age of three hours
Between our after-supper and bedtime?
Where is our usual manager of mirth?
What revels are in hand? Is there no play
To ease the anguish of a torturing hour?
Call Philostrate.

PHILOSTRATE　　　Here, mighty Theseus.

THESEUS

Say, what abridgement have you for this evening?
40 What masque, what music? How shall we beguile
The lazy time if not with some delight?

PHILOSTRATE (*giving a paper*)

There is a brief how many sports are ripe.
Make choice of which your highness will see first.

THESEUS

The Battle with the Centaurs, 'to be sung
By an Athenian eunuch to the harp'.
We'll none of that. That have I told my love
In glory of my kinsman, Hercules.
The riot of the tipsy Bacchanals,
Tearing the Thracian singer in their rage.
50 That is an old device, and it was played
When I from Thebes came last a conqueror.
The thrice three Muses mourning for the death
Of learning, late deceased in beggary.
That is some satire keen and critical,

Not sorting with a nuptial ceremony.
A tedious brief scene of young Pyramus
And his love Thisbe; 'very tragical mirth'.
Merry and tragical? Tedious and brief?
That is, hot ice and wondrous strange snow.
How shall we find the concord of this discord? 60

PHILOSTRATE
A play there is, my lord, some ten words long,
Which is as 'brief' as I have known a play.
But by ten words, my lord, it is too long,
Which makes it 'tedious'. For in all the play
There is not one word apt, one player fitted.
And 'tragical', my noble lord, it is,
For Pyramus therein doth kill himself,
Which when I saw rehearsed, I must confess,
Made mine eyes water: but more 'merry' tears
The passion of loud laughter never shed. 70

THESEUS
What are they that do play it?

PHILOSTRATE
Hard-handed men that work in Athens here,
Which never laboured in their minds till now,
And now have toiled their unbreathed memories
With this same play against your nuptial.

THESEUS
And we will hear it.

PHILOSTRATE   No, my noble lord,
It is not for you. I have heard it over,
And it is nothing, nothing in the world,
Unless you can find sport in their intents,
Extremely stretched, and conned with cruel pain, 80
To do you service.

THESEUS   I will hear that play,
For never anything can be amiss

When simpleness and duty tender it.
Go bring them in; and take your places, ladies.

Exit Philostrate

HIPPOLYTA

I love not to see wretchedness o'ercharged,
And duty in his service perishing.

THESEUS

Why, gentle sweet, you shall see no such thing.

HIPPOLYTA

He says they can do nothing in this kind.

THESEUS

The kinder we, to give them thanks for nothing.
90 Our sport shall be to take what they mistake;
And what poor duty cannot do, noble respect
Takes it in might, not merit.
Where I have come, great clerks have purposèd
To greet me with premeditated welcomes,
Where I have seen them shiver and look pale,
Make periods in the midst of sentences,
Throttle their practised accent in their fears,
And in conclusion dumbly have broke off,
Not paying me a welcome. Trust me, sweet,
100 Out of this silence yet I picked a welcome,
And in the modesty of fearful duty
I read as much as from the rattling tongue
Of saucy and audacious eloquence.
Love, therefore, and tongue-tied simplicity
In least speak most, to my capacity.

Enter Philostrate

PHILOSTRATE

So please your grace, the Prologue is addressed.

THESEUS Let him approach.

Flourish of trumpets
Enter Quince as Prologue

QUINCE

If we offend it is with our good will.
That you should think we come not to offend
But with good will. To show our simple skill,　　　110
That is the true beginning of our end.
Consider then we come but in despite.
We do not come as minding to content you,
Our true intent is. All for your delight
We are not here. That you should here repent you
The actors are at hand, and by their show
You shall know all that you are like to know.

THESEUS This fellow doth not stand upon points.

LYSANDER He hath rid his prologue like a rough colt; he
knows not the stop. A good moral, my lord: it is not　120
enough to speak, but to speak true.

HIPPOLYTA Indeed, he hath played on his prologue like a
child on a recorder – a sound, but not in government.

THESEUS His speech was like a tangled chain: nothing
impaired, but all disordered. Who is next?

> *Enter Bottom as Pyramus, Flute as Thisbe, Snout as*
> *Wall, Starveling as Moonshine, and Snug as Lion;*
> *a trumpeter before them*

QUINCE

Gentles, perchance you wonder at this show;
But wonder on, till truth make all things plain.
This man is Pyramus, if you would know;
This beauteous lady Thisbe is, certain.
This man with lime and roughcast doth present　　　130
Wall – that vile wall which did these lovers sunder;
And through Wall's chink, poor souls, they are content
To whisper. At the which let no man wonder.
This man with lantern, dog, and bush of thorn
Presenteth Moonshine. For if you will know
By moonshine did these lovers think no scorn

To meet at Ninus' tomb, there, there to woo.
This grisly beast – which Lion hight by name –
The trusty Thisbe coming first by night
140 Did scare away, or rather did affright.
And as she fled, her mantle she did fall,
  Which Lion vile with bloody mouth did stain.
Anon comes Pyramus – sweet youth and tall –
  And finds his trusty Thisbe's mantle slain.
Whereat with blade – with bloody, blameful blade –
  He bravely broached his boiling bloody breast.
And Thisbe, tarrying in mulberry shade,
  His dagger drew, and died. For all the rest,
Let Lion, Moonshine, Wall, and lovers twain
150 At large discourse while here they do remain.

Exeunt Quince, Bottom, Flute, Snug, and Starveling

THESEUS
I wonder if the lion be to speak.
DEMETRIUS
No wonder, my lord – one lion may, when many asses do.
SNOUT *as Wall*
In this same interlude it doth befall
That I – one Snout by name – present a wall.
And such a wall as I would have you think
That had in it a crannied hole or chink,
Through which the lovers, Pyramus and Thisbe,
Did whisper often, very secretly.
This loam, this roughcast, and this stone doth show
160 That I am that same wall; the truth is so.
And this the cranny is, right and sinister,
Through which the fearful lovers are to whisper.
THESEUS Would you desire lime and hair to speak better?
DEMETRIUS It is the wittiest partition that ever I heard
discourse, my lord.

Enter Bottom as Pyramus

THESEUS Pyramus draws near the wall. Silence!

BOTTOM *as Pyramus*

O grim-looked night, O night with hue so black,
  O night which ever art when day is not!
O night, O night, alack, alack, alack,
  I fear my Thisbe's promise is forgot.   170
And thou, O wall, O sweet, O lovely wall,
  That standest between her father's ground and mine,
Thou wall, O wall, O sweet and lovely wall,
  Show me thy chink to blink through with mine eyne.
    Wall holds up his fingers
Thanks, courteous wall; Jove shield thee well for this.
  But what see I? No Thisbe do I see.
O wicked wall, through whom I see no bliss:
  Cursed be thy stones for thus deceiving me!

THESEUS The wall, methinks, being sensible, should curse
  again.   180

BOTTOM No, in truth sir, he should not. 'Deceiving me' is
  Thisbe's cue. She is to enter now, and I am to spy her
  through the wall. You shall see – it will fall pat as I told
  you. Yonder she comes.
    Enter Flute as Thisbe

FLUTE *as Thisbe*

O wall, full often hast thou heard my moans
  For parting my fair Pyramus and me.
My cherry lips have often kissed thy stones,
  Thy stones with lime and hair knit up in thee.

BOTTOM *as Pyramus*

I see a voice. Now will I to the chink
  To spy an I can hear my Thisbe's face.   190
Thisbe!

FLUTE *as Thisbe*

          My love! Thou art my love, I think?

113

BOTTOM *as Pyramus*

    Think what thou wilt, I am thy lover's grace,
And like Limander am I trusty still.

FLUTE *as Thisbe*

And I like Helen till the Fates me kill.

BOTTOM *as Pyramus*

Not Shafalus to Procrus was so true.

FLUTE *as Thisbe*

    As Shafalus to Procrus, I to you.

BOTTOM *as Pyramus*

    O, kiss me through the hole of this vile wall!

FLUTE *as Thisbe*

I kiss the wall's hole, not your lips at all.

BOTTOM *as Pyramus*

Wilt thou at Ninny's tomb meet me straight way?

FLUTE *as Thisbe*

200   Tide life, tide death, I come without delay.

                      Exeunt Bottom and Flute

SNOUT *as Wall*

Thus have I, Wall, my part dischargèd so;
And being done, thus Wall away doth go.   *Exit*

THESEUS Now is the mural down between the two neigh-
    bours.

DEMETRIUS No remedy, my lord, when walls are so wilful
    to hear without warning.

HIPPOLYTA This is the silliest stuff that ever I heard.

THESEUS The best in this kind are but shadows; and the
    worst are no worse, if imagination amend them.

210 HIPPOLYTA It must be your imagination, then, and not
    theirs.

THESEUS If we imagine no worse of them than they of
    themselves, they may pass for excellent men. Here come
    two noble beasts in: a man and a lion.

    Enter Snug as Lion and Starveling as Moonshine

SNUG *as Lion*
> You, ladies – you whose gentle hearts do fear
> > The smallest monstrous mouse that creeps on floor –
> May now, perchance, both quake and tremble here,
> > When Lion rough in wildest rage doth roar.
> Then know that I as Snug the joiner am
> A lion fell, nor else no lion's dam,
> For if I should as lion come in strife
> Into this place, 'twere pity on my life.

THESEUS A very gentle beast, and of a good conscience.

DEMETRIUS The very best at a beast, my lord, that e'er I saw.

LYSANDER This lion is a very fox for his valour.

THESEUS True; and a goose for his discretion.

DEMETRIUS Not so, my lord; for his valour cannot carry his discretion; and the fox carries the goose.

THESEUS His discretion, I am sure, cannot carry his valour; for the goose carries not the fox. It is well: leave it to his discretion, and let us listen to the moon.

STARVELING *as Moonshine*
> This lanthorn doth the hornèd moon present.

DEMETRIUS He should have worn the horns on his head.

THESEUS He is no crescent, and his horns are invisible within the circumference.

STARVELING *as Moonshine*
> This lanthorn doth the hornèd moon present;
> > Myself the man i'th'moon do seem to be.

THESEUS This is the greatest error of all the rest; the man should be put into the lantern. How is it else the man i'th'moon?

DEMETRIUS He dares not come there, for the candle. For, you see, it is already in snuff.

HIPPOLYTA I am aweary of this moon. Would he would change.

THESEUS It appears by his small light of discretion that
he is in the wane. But yet in courtesy, in all reason, we
must stay the time.

LYSANDER Proceed, Moon.

250 STARVELING All that I have to say is to tell you that the
lantern is the moon, I the man i'th'moon, this thorn
bush my thorn bush, and this dog my dog.

DEMETRIUS Why, all these should be in the lantern; for
all these are in the moon. But silence: here comes Thisbe.

Enter Flute as Thisbe

FLUTE *as Thisbe*

This is old Ninny's tomb. Where is my love?

SNUG *as Lion*

O!

Lion roars. Flute as Thisbe runs off

DEMETRIUS Well roared, Lion!

THESEUS Well run, Thisbe!

HIPPOLYTA Well shone, Moon! Truly, the moon shines
260 with a good grace.

Lion tears Thisbe's mantle. Exit

THESEUS Well moused, Lion!

DEMETRIUS And then came Pyramus.

LYSANDER And so the lion vanished.

Enter Bottom as Pyramus

BOTTOM *as Pyramus*

Sweet moon, I thank thee for thy sunny beams;
I thank thee, moon, for shining now so bright;
For by thy gracious, golden, glittering beams
I trust to take of truest Thisbe sight.
But stay – O spite!
But mark, poor Knight,
270 What dreadful dole is here?
Eyes, do you see? –
How can it be?

116

       O dainty duck, O dear!
        Thy mantle good –
        What, stained with blood!
       Approach, ye Furies fell.
         O Fates, come, come,
         Cut thread and thrum,
          Quail, crush, conclude, and quell.

THESEUS This passion, and the death of a dear friend, 280
would go near to make a man look sad.

HIPPOLYTA Beshrew my heart, but I pity the man.

BOTTOM *as Pyramus*
  O wherefore, nature, didst thou lions frame,
    Since lion vile hath here deflowered my dear?
  Which is – no, no, which was – the fairest dame
    That lived, that loved, that liked, that looked with cheer.
        Come tears, confound;
        Out sword, and wound
       The pap of Pyramus.
        Ay, that left pap,   290
        Where heart doth hop.
       Thus die I – thus, thus, thus.

He stabs himself
        Now am I dead,
        Now am I fled;
      My soul is in the sky.
        Tongue, lose thy light;
        Moon, take thy flight;
               Exit Starveling as Moonshine
       Now die, die, die, die, die.   *He dies*

DEMETRIUS No die, but an ace for him; for he is but one.

LYSANDER Less than an ace, man; for he is dead. He is 300
nothing.

THESEUS With the help of a surgeon he might yet recover,
and prove an ass.

HIPPOLYTA How chance Moonshine is gone before
Thisbe comes back and finds her lover?

THESEUS She will find him by starlight. Here she comes;
and her passion ends the play.

Enter Flute as Thisbe

HIPPOLYTA Methinks she should not use a long one for
such a Pyramus. I hope she will be brief.

310 DEMETRIUS A mote will turn the balance which Pyramus,
which Thisbe is the better – he for a man, God warrant
us; she for a woman, God bless us.

LYSANDER She hath spied him already, with those sweet
eyes.

DEMETRIUS And thus she means, videlicet:

FLUTE *as Thisbe*

Asleep, my love?
What, dead, my dove?
O Pyramus, arise.
Speak, speak. Quite dumb?
320   Dead, dead? A tomb
Must cover thy sweet eyes.
These lily lips,
This cherry nose,
These yellow cowslip cheeks
Are gone, are gone.
Lovers, make moan –
His eyes were green as leeks.
O sisters three,
Come, come to me
330   With hands as pale as milk;
Lay them in gore,
Since you have shore
With shears his thread of silk.
Tongue, not a word!
Come, trusty sword,

>   Come blade, my breast imbrue.
>   *She stabs herself*
>   And farewell friends.
>   Thus Thisbe ends.
>   Adieu, adieu, adieu!

>   *She dies*

THESEUS Moonshine and Lion are left to bury the dead.   340

DEMETRIUS Ay, and Wall, too.

BOTTOM (*starting up*) No, I assure you, the wall is down
that parted their fathers. Will it please you to see the
epilogue, or to hear a Bergomask dance between two of
our company?

THESEUS No epilogue, I pray you; for your play needs no
excuse. Never excuse; for when the players are all dead,
there need none to be blamed. Marry, if he that writ it
had played Pyramus and hanged himself in Thisbe's
garter, it would have been a fine tragedy. And so it is,   350
truly, and very notably discharged. But come, your
Bergomask; let your epilogue alone.

>   *A dance. Exeunt Bottom and his fellows*
> The iron tongue of midnight hath told twelve.
> Lovers, to bed; 'tis almost fairy time.
> I fear we shall outsleep the coming morn
> As much as we this night have overwatched.
> This palpable-gross play hath well beguiled
> The heavy gait of night. Sweet friends, to bed.
> A fortnight hold we this solemnity
> In nightly revels and new jollity.   360

>   *Exeunt Theseus, Hippolyta, Philostrate,*
>   *Demetrius, Helena, Lysander, Hermia,*
>   *Lords, and Attendants*

>   *Enter Puck*

PUCK
>   Now the hungry lion roars

And the wolf behowls the moon,
Whilst the heavy ploughman snores
All with weary task foredone.
Now the wasted brands do glow
Whilst the screech-owl, screeching loud,
Puts the wretch that lies in woe
In remembrance of a shroud.
Now it is the time of night
370   That the graves, all gaping wide,
Every one lets forth his sprite
In the churchway paths to glide.
And we fairies, that do run
By the triple Hecate's team,
From the presence of the sun
Following darkness like a dream,
Now are frolic. Not a mouse
Shall disturb this hallowed house.
I am sent with broom before
380   To sweep the dust behind the door.
   Enter Oberon and Titania, with all their train

OBERON

Through the house give glimmering light
By the dead and drowsy fire;
Every elf and fairy sprite
Hop as light as bird from briar,
And this ditty after me
Sing, and dance it trippingly.

TITANIA

First rehearse your song by rote,
To each word a warbling note.
Hand in hand with fairy grace
390   Will we sing and bless this place.
   Song and dance

OBERON

Now until the break of day
Through this house each fairy stray.
To the best bride bed will we,
Which by us shall blessèd be;
And the issue there create
Ever shall be fortunate.
So shall all the couples three
Ever true in loving be,
And the blots of nature's hand
Shall not in their issue stand. 400
Never mole, harelip, nor scar,
Nor mark prodigious, such as are
Despisèd in nativity,
Shall upon their children be.
With this field dew consecrate
Every fairy take his gait,
And each several chamber bless
Through this palace with sweet peace;
And the owner of it blessed
Ever shall in safety rest. 410
Trip away; make no stay.
Meet me all by break of day.

Exeunt Oberon, Titania, and their train

PUCK (*to the audience*)

If we shadows have offended,
Think but this, and all is mended:
That you have but slumbered here
While these visions did appear.
And this weak and idle theme,
No more yielding but a dream,
Gentles, do not reprehend.
If you pardon, we will mend. 420
And, as I am an honest Puck,

If we have unearnèd luck
Now to scape the serpent's tongue
We will make amends ere long,
Else the Puck a liar call.
So, good night unto you all.
Give me your hands if we be friends,
And Robin shall restore amends.   *Exit*

COMMENTARY

THE Act and scene divisions are those of Peter Alexander's edition of the *Complete Works*, London, 1951. All references to other plays by Shakespeare are to this edition.

In the Commentary and the Account of the Text, the first Quarto (1600) is referred to as Q1, the second Quarto (1619) as Q2, both Quartos as Q, and the first Folio (1623) as F. For further details, see the Account of the Text. In quotations from the Quartos and the Folio the 'long s' (ʃ) has been replaced by 's'.

The title
'Midsummer Night' is 23 June. In Act Four, Theseus suggests that the lovers 'rose up early to observe | The rite of May' (IV.1.131–2). 'Maying' was not confined to 1 May; it could happen at various times. The title suggests the traditional magic associations of midsummer, and also perhaps the fact that then were practised folk-customs by which young people were supposed to be able to discover whom they were going to marry. The play's action is spread over only two days, though Shakespeare suggests at the start that it will last four days.

I   The Elizabethan stage used little or no scenery. The dramatist could specify the location of a scene if he wished, but could also leave it unmentioned. Many of Shakespeare's scenes depend for their effect partly on our consciousness that they are being enacted on a stage, rather than on our succumbing totally to the illusion that they happen in the place mentioned. With this reservation, the first scene takes place somewhere in Athens.

4   *lingers* delays

6 *withering out* causing to dwindle. The idea is that the young man has inherited his father's estate, but has to go on paying some of the income to the widow.

7 *steep themselves* be absorbed

13 *pert* lively, brisk

15 *companion* fellow (used contemptuously)
  pomp procession, pageant, ceremony

16–17 *Hippolyta, I wooed thee with my sword,* | *And won thy love doing thee injuries.* Theseus captured Hippolyta in conquering the Amazons.

19 *triumph* public festivity and show of rejoicing
  (stage direction) *Egeus* (pronounced Egee-us: three syllables)
  Hermia. We learn from III.2.257 and 288 that Hermia is short and dark.

24, 26 *Stand forth, Demetrius!* and *Stand forth, Lysander!* are printed as stage directions in the early editions. The fact that they complete the verse lines shows that they should be spoken.

32 *stolen the impression of her fantasy* craftily impressed yourself on her fancy. Obviously the metre demands some elision. The actor is likely to pronounce 'stolen' as one syllable ('stol'n') and 'the impression' as three ('th'impression'). There are many other examples in the play of unaccented or lightly accented syllables in verse lines. Editors frequently mark such syllables with an apostrophe. But Shakespeare's verse does not conform to a mathematically exact system of versification, and we cannot always be sure whether for instance an un-accented syllable at the end of a line should be sounded or not (III.2.345: 'This is thy negligence. Still thou mistakest'). Also the marking of such syllables may suggest an abruptness of speaking which is neither necessary nor desirable. For instance, II.1.191 reads 'Thou toldest me they were stolen unto this wood'. Obviously the second syllable in 'toldest' and 'stolen' will be very lightly stressed. Yet an actor may find it

easier to sound the syllables while preserving the rhythm rather than try to pronounce something printed as 'told'st' and 'stol'n'. For these reasons, unaccented syllables that may have been elided for metrical reasons are generally printed in full in the present edition.

33 *gauds* playthings, toys
conceits fancy things, trinkets

34 *Knacks* knick-knacks

35 *prevailment* power

39 *Be it so* if

45 *Immediately* expressly

54 *in this kind* in this respect
voice approval, favour

56-7 *my eyes . . . his judgement.* The play is to be much concerned with troubles caused by a dislocation between the evidence of the senses and the reasoning power. See Introduction, pages 27-32.

60 *concern* befit

65 *die the death* be put to death by legal process

68, 74 *blood* passions, feelings

70 *livery* habit, costume

71 *For aye* for ever
mewed confined

73 *moon* (as Diana, goddess of chastity)

76 *earthlier happy* happier on earth
rose distilled. Roses were distilled to make perfumes.

80 *patent* privilege

81 *his lordship* (that is, the lordship of him; the metrical stress is on 'his')

92 *crazèd title* flawed, unsound claim

98 *estate unto* settle, bestow upon

99-110 *I am, my lord. . . .* Shaw, in the review quoted from in the Introduction (page 10), writes: 'it should be clear to any stage manager that Lysander's speech, beginning "I am, my lord, as well derived as he", should be spoken privately and not publicly to Theseus.'

99 *derived* descended

100 *well possessed* rich

101 *My fortunes every way as fairly ranked* my fortunes [are] of as good a rank. (Abbreviation was not always clearly indicated by Elizabethan printers, so it may be that we should read *My fortune's*.)

102 *with vantage* better

106 *to his head* to his face, in his teeth

110 *spotted* stained, polluted

117 *arm* prepare

120 *extenuate* mitigate, relax

123 *go along* come along with me

124 *business* (pronounced with three syllables)

125 *Against* in preparation for

126 *nearly that concerns* that closely concerns

130 *Belike* perhaps

131 *Beteem* allow

134–40 *The course of true love.* . . . Shaw, in the review quoted from in the Introduction (page 10), comments: 'Shakespeare makes the two star-crossed lovers speak in alternate lines with an effect which sets the whole scene throbbing with their absorption in one another.'

135 *blood* birth, rank

137 *misgraffèd* badly matched

143 *momentany* (an obsolete form of 'momentary')

145 *collied* blackened, darkened

146 *spleen* impulse; fit of anger or passion

149 *quick.* This may be taken either as an adjective (alive, vital) or an adverb (quickly).

155 *fancy* love

156 *persuasion* principle, doctrine

158 *revenue* (pronounced here with the accent on the second syllable)

159–60 *From Athens is her house remote seven leagues; | And she respects me as her only son.* Dr Johnson and some later editors reverse the order of these lines. This may be an improvement in fluency, but it brings together two

126

clauses beginning with 'and', which seems clumsy.
There is no need for the alteration.

165 *without* outside

167 *To do observance to a morn of May* to celebrate May-day.
The celebrations, common in Elizabethan times, if not
in the classical ones in which the action is ostensibly
set, generally took place in the woods outside a town.

170 *his best arrow with the golden head.* Cupid was said to
carry arrows of lead to repel love, and arrows of gold to
cause it. The legend is given in Ovid's *Metamorphoses*,
well known to Shakespeare, and anyhow was common
knowledge.

171 *By the simplicity of Venus' doves.* . . . Hermia moves from
blank verse into rhyming couplets for her vow. The
remainder of the scene is in couplets.
simplicity innocence, guilelessness
Venus' doves. Doves were sacred to Venus, and drew her
car. The last stanza of Shakespeare's *Venus and Adonis*,
written in 1593, within a year or two of *A Midsummer
Night's Dream*, is:

> *Thus weary of the world, away she hies,*
> *And yokes her silver doves, by whose swift aid*
> *Their mistress, mounted, through the empty skies*
> *In her light chariot quickly is conveyed;*
> *Holding their course to Paphos, where their queen*
> *Means to immure herself and not be seen.*

173-4 *fire which burned the Carthage queen | When the false
Trojan under sail was seen.* Dido, Queen of Carthage,
burned herself on a funeral pyre when her lover, the
Trojan Aeneas, sailed away. The story is told by Virgil
in the *Aeneid*, and is the subject of a play by Marlowe
and Nashe dating probably from a few years before
A Midsummer Night's Dream.

179 *Helena.* We learn from III.2.187 and 291–3 that Helena
is tall and fair.

182 *fair* beauty, kind of beauty. The Folio reads 'you

127

fair', which makes equally good sense; but the Quarto reading is more likely to be Shakespeare's.

183   *lodestars* leading or guiding stars

184   *tuneable* tuneful, musical

186   *favour* good looks

190   *bated* excepted

191   *translated* transformed

207   *That he hath turned a heaven unto a hell?* This notion is varied at II.1.243–4, when Helena says of Demetrius:

> *I'll follow thee, and make a heaven of hell,*
> *To die upon the hand I love so well.*

209   *Phoebe* (the moon)

212   *still* always

213   *Athens.* The noun is used as an adjective, as in 'the Carthage queen' (line 173).

214–21 *where often you and I. . . .* The reference to the girlhood friendship of Hermia and Helena looks forward to the scene of their quarrel, to which it is an ironic background.

219   *stranger companies* the company of strangers. The early editions read 'strange companions'. A rhyme to 'eyes' is required.

223   *lovers' food* (the sight of each other)

226   *other some* some others

232–3 *Things base and vile, holding no quantity,* | *Love can transpose to form and dignity.* This looks forward especially to Titania's infatuation with Bottom.

232   *quantity* proportion

234   *Love looks not with the eyes, but with the mind.* That is, love is prompted not by the objective evidence of the senses, but by the fancies of the mind.

237   *figure* symbolize, represent

240   *waggish* playful

242   *eyne* eyes (an old form, common in Shakespeare, especially in rhymed passages)

248   *intelligence* news, information

249   *a dear expense* (perhaps 'an expense of trouble worth making', or possibly 'it will cost him dear', that is, 'merely to thank me will be painful to him')

2   As is common in Shakespeare and in Elizabethan plays generally, the characters of low social standing speak in prose. No particular location for this scene is suggested. It takes place somewhere in Athens.

   (stage direction) *Bottom.* As a weaver's term, a bottom was the object on which thread was wound. 'Bottom' as 'posterior' is not recorded till late in the eighteenth century, but the name 'Mistress Frigbottom' in Thomas Dekker's *The Shoemaker's Holiday* (1600) shows that this sense existed in Shakespeare's time. *Starveling.* Tailors were proverbially thin.

2   *generally* (Bottom's mistaken way of saying 'severally', that is, individually)

5   *interlude* play

11–12   *The most lamentable comedy.* . . . The title of the mechanicals' play parodies ones such as *A lamentable tragedy mixed full of pleasant mirth, containing the life of Cambyses, King of Persia*, published about 1570. See also V.1.56–7, where the play is described as '*A tedious brief scene of young Pyramus | And his love Thisbe;* "very tragical mirth" '.

15   *Masters, spread yourselves.* It is not clear exactly what action is intended here. Some producers have the mechanicals seated on a bench.

24   *condole* lament, express grief

25   *humour* inclination, fancy

26   *Ercles* Hercules. This may allude to a ranting role in a particular play, now lost.

   part to tear a cat in. The phrase, proverbial now for a ranting role, may have been so in Shakespeare's time.

27–34   *The raging rocks.* . . . This may be a quotation from a lost play. More probably it is Shakespeare's burlesque of the kind of writing found in two somewhat similar

passages of John Studley's translation (1581) of
Seneca's *Hercules Oetaeus*:

> *O lord of ghosts, whose fiery flash*
> > *That forth thy hand doth shake*
> *Doth cause the trembling lodges twain*
> > *Of Phoebus' car to quake . . .*
> *The roaring rocks have quaking stirred,*
> > *And none thereat hath pushed;*
> *Hell gloomy gates I have brast ope*
> > *Where grisly ghosts all hushed*
> *Have stood.*

31   *Phibbus' car* the chariot of Phoebus, the sun-god.
'Phibbus', Q1's spelling, may represent Bottom's idiosyncratic pronunciation.

37   *condoling* pathetic

41   *a wandering knight* a knight-errant (a typical role in a
play)

43   *let not me play a woman* (a reminder that women's parts
were played by boys and young men in Shakespeare's
time)

45   *mask* (a customary item of ladies' costume in Shakespeare's time)

47   *An* if

48   *Thisne*. Probably the spelling represents Bottom's pronunciation. But some commentators believe that
Shakespeare wrote *thisne*, meaning 'in this manner'.
The word is not found elsewhere in Shakespeare's
writings.

56–9 *Thisbe's mother . . . , Pyramus' father . . . Thisbe's father.*
These characters do not appear in the play as acted.
There are other discrepancies between the play as projected and as performed. A realistic explanation should
not be sought.

76   *aggravate*. Bottom means 'moderate'. Mistress Quickly
makes the same error (*2 Henry IV*, II.4.153): 'I
beseek you now, aggravate your choler.'

77   *roar you* (a colloquialism: 'roar for you', or simply 'roar')

       sucking unweaned

78   *an 'twere* as if it were

80   *proper* handsome

83–9   *What beard were I best to play it in? . . .* Bottom's interest in the colour of beards is perhaps appropriate to his craft of weaver.

87   *orange-tawny* dark yellow

       purple-in-grain dyed with a fast purple or red

88   *French-crown-colour* light yellow like a gold coin. (The French *écu* seems to be alluded to mainly for the sake of the joke that follows.)

90   *crowns* heads. 'French crown' refers to the baldness produced by venereal disease, particularly associated by the English with France.

97   *properties* stage requisites

100   *obscenely*. The point lies rather in the unfitness of this word than in what Bottom intended. He may have meant 'seemly'. Compare Costard in *Love's Labour's Lost*, IV.1.136: 'When it comes so smoothly off, so obscenely, as it were, so fit.'

       be perfect know your lines.

103   *hold, or cut bowstrings*. This is an expression in archery of uncertain meaning. It is reasonably interpreted as 'Keep your promise or be disgraced.'

.1   With this scene the play moves into the wood. It is the night of Lysander's and Hermia's attempt to escape from Athens, that is, 'tomorrow night' in relation to the first scene. The rhyming verse used for the opening conversation between Puck and the Fairy forms an immediate contrast with the mechanicals' prose.

       (stage direction) *at one door . . . at another* (a common direction in Elizabethan plays, referring to the doors at the sides of the stage)

Puck. Puck is often referred to in stage directions and speech prefixes of the early editions as Robin Good-fellow, and is so spoken of and addressed in the dialogue. A 'puck' is a devil or an imp. Properly the character in the play is Robin Goodfellow, a puck.

Robin Goodfellow's appearance is described in a stage direction of *Grim the Collier of Croydon*, a play of unknown authorship written about 1600: 'Enter Robin Goodfellow, in a suit of leather close to his body; his face and hands coloured russet-colour, with a flail.'

2   *Over hill, over dale*. . . . The Fairy (commonly played by a young woman in modern productions, but presumably by a boy in Shakespeare's time) is given a new verse form.

4   *pale* fenced land, park. (That is, the fairies wander over both public and private land.)

7   *moon's sphere*. According to the astronomical notions of Shakespeare's day, the moon was fixed in a hollow crystalline sphere or globe which itself revolved round the earth each twenty-four hours.

9   *orbs* fairy rings – circles of darker grass

10   *pensioners*. Queen Elizabeth was attended by fifty handsome young gentlemen-pensioners, her royal bodyguard, who were splendidly dressed. The word carries no implications of poverty.

16   *lob* clown, lout. (Puck is clearly among the least ethereal of fairies.)

17   *elves* fairy boys. (That is, presumably, Cobweb, Peaseblossom, Moth, and Mustardseed.)

20   *passing* exceedingly
      fell fierce, angry

22   *Indian*. Oberon and Titania are again associated with India at lines 69 and 124.

      Titania gives a different account of the boy (lines 123–37).

23   *changeling* (usually a child left by fairies in exchange for

one stolen, but here, the stolen child. The word has
three syllables.)

25   *trace* range, track through

26   *perforce* by force

29   *starlight sheen* shining light of the stars

30   *square* quarrel

32   *making* form, shape, build

33   *shrewd* mischievous

35   *villagery* villages

36   *Skim milk* steal cream

    quern hand-mill for grinding corn. Puck is either grind-
ing meal himself or mischievously labouring to cause
the grinding to fail.

37   *bootless* fruitlessly. (Puck prevents the milk from turning
to butter.)

38   *barm* froth on ale

39   *Mislead* (that is, with false fire. Puck later (III.1.103–5)
declares his intention of doing this to the mechanicals.)

40   *Hobgoblin* (another name for Robin Goodfellow)

45   *bean-fed*. Field beans were used as food for horses, and
were also known as horse-beans.

    beguile trick

47   *gossip* old woman, crony

48   *crab* crab-apple; an ingredient in a drink

50   *dewlap* skin hanging from the neck; or (possibly) breasts

51   *aunt* old woman, gossip

    saddest most serious

54   *And 'Tailor' cries*. The exact meaning is unknown.
Dr Johnson writes: 'The custom of crying "tailor" at a
sudden fall backwards I think I remember to have ob-
served. He that slips beside his chair falls as a tailor
squats upon his board.' *Tailor* may mean 'posterior'.

55   *choir* company

56   *waxen* increase

    neeze sneeze

57   *wasted* spent

59   (stage direction) *Titania*. In the classical pronunciation

(which Shakespeare probably followed) the first two vowels would be long: that is, the first syllable would be pronounced 'tight', and the name would rhyme with 'mania'.

60 *Ill met by moonlight, proud Titania!* ... The entrance of Titania and Oberon is marked by a change from rhyming to blank verse.

61 *Fairy, skip hence.* This is often emended to 'Fairies'; but Titania may be addressing the Fairy who has been speaking to Oberon's follower, Puck.

64–5 *know* | *When* know of occasions when

66, 68 *Corin* ... *Phillida* (type-names of the love-sick shepherd and his beloved)

69 *step.* Perhaps 'limit of travel or exploration', resembling the phrase in *Much Ado About Nothing* (II.1.237): 'I will fetch you a tooth-picker now from the furthest inch of Asia.' 'Steppe', meaning a great plain, was probably not a known word at the time. Q2 and F read 'steepe', which may be correct, referring to a mountain, perhaps of the Himalayas.

70 *Amazon* (that is, Hippolyta, Queen of the Amazons)

71 *buskined* wearing hunting boots. Hippolyta was known as a huntress.

75 *Glance at* hit at, reflect upon

78–80 *Perigenia* ... *Aegles* ... *Ariadne* ... *Antiopa.* All loved by Theseus. Shakespeare seems to have taken the names from Plutarch's *Life of Theseus*, where the first appears as 'Perigouna'.

80 *Ariadne.* The legend of Ariadne's helping Theseus to thread the labyrinth in which the Minotaur was confined, and his deserting her, was well known.

81–117 *These are the forgeries of jealousy....* This speech is commented on in the Introduction, pages 12, 24–5.

82 *middle summer's spring* the beginning ('spring') of midsummer

84 *pavèd* pebbled

85 *in* on

margent shore

86 *ringlets* dances in the form of a ring (the meaning 'lock of hair' is not recorded before 1667)

to to the sound of

90 *Contagious* pestilential, harmful

91 *pelting* paltry

92 *continents* banks

97 *murrion flock* flock infected with murrion (or 'murrain'), a disease of sheep and cattle

98 *nine men's morris* area marked out in squares for the game of the same name, a sort of open-air draughts, in which each player has nine pieces

99 *quaint mazes* intricate arrangements of paths, normally kept visible by being frequently trodden

wanton green luxuriant grass

101 *cheer* (a commonly accepted emendation for 'here' in the early editions, which may however be correct. 'Here' seems weak, whereas 'cheer' would look forward to the following line)

103 *Therefore.* This repeats the 'Therefore' of line 88.

104 *washes* moistens, wets

105 *rheumatic* characterized by 'rheum', that is, colds, coughs, etc. (The accent is on the first syllable.)

106 *distemperature.* The word means both 'ill-humour, discomposure' and 'bad weather'.

109 *Hiems* winter personified. He is introduced into the closing episode of *Love's Labour's Lost* (V.2.878): 'This side is Hiems, Winter; this Ver, the Spring'.

112 *childing* fertile, fruitful (autumn as the season of harvest)

change exchange

113 *wonted* customary

mazèd amazed, bewildered

114 *increase* (seasonal) products

116 *debate* quarrel

123 *votaress* a woman under vow (in Titania's 'order')

127 *traders* trading ships

140 *round* round dance

135

142   *spare* avoid

144–5   *Not for thy fairy kingdom!* ... As often, a couplet is
        used to mark the end of an episode.

145   *chide* quarrel

147   *injury* insult

149   *Since* when

151   *dulcet* sweet
        breath voice, song

152   *rude* rough

157   *certain* sure

158   *vestal* virgin (usually assumed to refer to Queen Eliza-
        beth)
        by in

159   *loveshaft* the golden arrow (compare I.1.170)

163   *And the imperial votaress passed on.* The scansion of this
        line is uncertain. The most satisfactory alternatives
        seem to be 'Ánd the impérial vót'ress pássèd ón' and
        'Ánd the impérial vótaréss páss'd ón'.
        imperial majestic, imperious, queenly

165   *bolt* arrow

168   *love in idleness* pansy or heart's ease. The idea that it
        changed from white to purple may have been suggested
        by Ovid's statement in the Pyramus and Thisbe story
        that the mulberry, once 'white as snow', was turned to
        'a deep dark purple colour' by Pyramus's blood.

171   *or ... or* either ... or

174   *leviathan* sea-monster; to the Elizabethans, a whale

176–87 *Having once this juice.* ... Oberon addresses the aud-
        ience.

192   *and wood* and mad

195   *adamant* very hard stone supposed to have magnetic
        properties

196–7   *But yet you draw not iron: for my heart | Is true as steel.*
        Iron is the obvious substance to be attracted by
        adamant; Helena stresses her more-than-ordinary
        fidelity to Demetrius. The conceit is somewhat strained,

perhaps with a deliberate effect of slightly comic inanity.

199   *speak you fair* speak kindly to you

214   *impeach* call in question, discredit

215   *To leave* by leaving

220   *Your virtue is my privilege.* A difficult expression. *Virtue* probably means 'qualities', 'attractions'. We may paraphrase: 'the effect of your qualities upon me puts me in a privileged position' – that is, because when Demetrius is there the night seems like day.

       For that because

224   *in my respect* to my mind

231   *Apollo flies, and Daphne holds the chase.* Daphne, flying from Apollo, was changed into a laurel tree so as to escape him. The story was familiar from Ovid's *Metamorphoses.*

232   *griffin* a fabulous monster with the body of a lion but the head, wings, and forehead of an eagle

       hind doe

233   *bootless* useless

235   *stay* wait for

240   *Your wrongs do set a scandal on my sex* the wrongs that you do me cause me to act in a manner that disgraces my sex

241   *We cannot fight for love.* . . . The scene moves into couplets, partly perhaps in preparation for Oberon's lyrical lines from line 249.

244   *upon* by

245   *Fare thee well, nymph.* Oberon, who has been an 'invisible' spectator, now comes forward.

250   *oxlips* flowering herbs, hybrids between the cowslip and the primrose

       grows (the singular verb with a plural subject was not unusual in Elizabethan English)

251   *woodbine* honeysuckle

252   *muskroses . . . eglantine* wild roses . . . sweet-briar

253   *some time* for some part of

255   *throws* throws off, casts

256   *Weed* garment

266   *fond on* in love, infatuated with

267   *ere the first cock crow*. Some supernatural beings were thought to be unable to bear daylight. At III.2.386 Oberon is dissociated from the ghosts and spirits who 'wilfully themselves exile from light'. This seems a way of stressing his generally benevolent function.

II.2   This scene follows immediately on the preceding one. The place is the bank mentioned by Oberon at II.1.249.

1   *roundel* round dance, all joining hands

2   *third part of a minute* (suggesting great rapidity of action on the part of the fairies)

4   *reremice* bats

7   *quaint* pretty, dainty

9   *double* forked

11   *Newts and blindworms*. Though neither is in fact harmful, they were thought to be so in Shakespeare's time. The witches' cauldron in *Macbeth* includes 'eye of newt' and 'blindworm's sting'.

13   *Philomel* the classical name for the nightingale

20   *spiders* (also thought to be poisonous)

21   *longlegged spinners* (probably daddylonglegs)

30   (stage direction) *Titania sleeps*. There is no break in the action between Titania's falling asleep and her awakening by Bottom at III.1.122. She must apparently remain on stage throughout this time. However, it is not necessary for her to be visible to the audience. It is possible that on the Elizabethan stage she occupied a recess that could be curtained off at the end of Oberon's spell (line 40), and that the curtain was drawn to reveal her during the first verse of Bottom's song (III.1.118).

32   *One aloof stand sentinel!* Perhaps on an Elizabethan stage one fairy would have been stationed on the upper stage ('aloof'). Oberon, whether or not his 'invisibility'

was effective with his fellow-fairies, would have been able to outwit the sentinel by confining his movements to the area at the back of the stage where, presumably, Titania sleeps. In stage practice, the sentinel is sometimes kidnapped by Oberon's attendants.

33–40 *What thou seest.* . . . Oberon's spell is distinguished by the use of trochaic, rhyming verse. This tripping measure is used elsewhere by fairy characters, e.g. the Fairy, II.1.6–13; Puck, II.2.72–89; Oberon for other spells at III.2.102–9 and IV.1.70–73, and Puck and Oberon in their following dialogue; Puck at III.2.396–9, 437–41; Puck, Oberon, and Titania at IV.1.92–101, and in the closing speeches, V.1.361–428.

36 *ounce* lynx

37 *Pard* leopard

48 *troth* (an old spelling of 'truth', preserved for the rhyme)

51 *take the sense* take the true meaning

52 *Love takes the meaning in love's conference.* In lovers' conversation ('conference') their love enables them truly to understand each other.

58 *lie* (a pun on the senses 'lie down' and 'deceive')

70 *Here is my bed* (that is, at some distance from Hermia)

74 *approve* test

76 *Who is here?* Puck mistakes Lysander for Demetrius.

78 *he my master said* he that my master said

85 *owe* own

92 *darkling* in darkness (the reminder was especially necessary in the open-air Elizabethan theatre)

94 *fond* foolish

95 *grace* answer to prayer

105 *sphery eyne* star-like eyes

110 *Transparent* (means both 'lacking in deceit; able to be seen through' and 'bright')
art magic power

120 *raven.* Compare III.2.257, where Lysander calls Hermia 'Ethiope'. She is presumably dark in hair or complexion.

121 *The will of man is by his reason swayed.* Lysander

ironically attributes to his reason the change in his
affections that has been brought about by Puck; see
Introduction, pages 26–7.

121 *will* desire

124 *ripe not* ('ripe' is a verb)

125 *And touching now the point of human skill* and I now
reaching the highest point of human capacity

127–8 *your eyes, where I o'erlook | Love's stories written in
love's richest book*. Shakespeare expresses a similar idea
in *Love's Labour's Lost* (IV.3.298–300):

> *From women's eyes this doctrine I derive:*
> *They are the ground, the books, the academes,*
> *From whence doth spring the true Promethean fire.*

127 *o'erlook* look over, read

138 *gentleness* nobility, breeding

139, 140 *of* by

145–6 *as the heresies that men do leave | Are hated most of those
they did deceive* as the heresies that men reject are hated
most by the very men who had been deceived by them

149 *address* direct, apply

156 *prey* preying

159 *an if* if

160 *of all loves* for love's sake

III.1 There is no break between the preceding scene and this
one.

  (stage direction) *clowns* rustics

2 *Pat* on the dot

4 *tiring-house* the dressing-room of the Elizabethan
theatre, directly behind the stage. On the Elizabethan
stage Bottom would have indicated the 'green plot' by
pointing to the stage, and the 'hawthorn brake' by
pointing to the tiring-house.

12 *By 'r lakin* by our Lady (a light oath)
  parlous perilous, terrible

16   *Write me* write (a colloquialism)

22   *eight and six* lines of eight and six syllables (a metre common in ballads)

27   *yourself.* The Folio has 'yourselves'; but the Quarto's singular form may well be a deliberate touch.

39   *it were pity of* it would be a bad thing for

46   SNUG. In the early editions the speech prefix is abbreviated to 'Sn.'. The line may be spoken by either Snug or Snout.

48   *find out moonshine!* The Folio has the stage direction 'Enter Puck' here. This conflicts with the entry given for him in the Folio and the Quarto at line 69. But it is possible that the Folio's apparently superfluous direction represents an early stage-practice of bringing Puck in to watch the mechanicals before he speaks.

51   *Great Chamber* state room

53-4 *bush of thorns.* A traditional attribute of the man in the moon, sometimes said to be the man who picked up a bundle of sticks on the Sabbath day (Numbers 15.32-6). There are other explanations. The following passage from Ben Jonson's masque *News from the New World* (1620), in reply to a report that a traveller from the moon has arrived on earth, is an appropriate comment:

FACTOR *Where? Which is he? I must see his dog at his girdle, and the bush of thorns at his back, ere I believe it.*
HERALD *These are stale ensigns of the stage's man in the moon.*

54   *disfigure* figure

71   *So near the cradle of the Fairy Queen?* (a reminder of Titania's presence)

72   *toward* in preparation

75-7 *flowers . . . sweet.* This passage is textually difficult. The Quartos read 'Odours, odorous' in line 76. The Folio reads 'Odours, odours'. The Folio reading, adopted here, may be interpreted to mean that Bottom ought to say 'the flowers of odours savours sweet' (taking

141

'savours' to mean 'savour'; the singular agreement with a plural subject would have been possible in Elizabethan English). Another possible explanation is that 'of' is a colloquialism for 'have'. If this were so, I should read 'Odorous, odorous' for Quince's correction of Bottom's 'odious'. This would have the advantage of fitting in better with 'hath' in 'so hath thy breath'.

81   *A stranger Pyramus than e'er played here.* Puck conceives the trick that he will play on Bottom.

88   *brisky juvenal* brisk youth (the diction is affected)
eke also (an old-fashioned word in Shakespeare's time)
Jew sometimes explained as an abbreviation of 'jewel' or 'juvenal', but perhaps no more than a deliberately inconsequential piece of padding

90   *Ninny's tomb.* A 'ninny' is a 'fool'. In Ovid's version of the story of Pyramus and Thisbe, they met at the tomb of Ninus, mythical founder of Nineveh.

93   *part* the script given to the actor, containing his speeches and cues

103   *headless bear.* Headless figures, whether human or animal, were traditional apparitions.
fire will o'the wisp

105   *at every turn.* The Folio has the stage direction 'Enter Piramus with the Asse head'. This seems to be a mistake; but it may be that Bottom goes out at the same time as the other mechanicals, and re-enters at this point.

112–13   *translated* transformed. This was a regular meaning; no joke is intended.

118–29   *The ousel cock.* . . . . Titania had been lulled to sleep with a song of the nightingale (Philomel). She is aroused by Bottom's song of more homely birds.

118   *ousel* blackbird

120   *throstle* thrush

121   *little quill* small voice

122   *What angel wakes me from my flowery bed?* If Titania has been curtained off during her sleep, she must re-

appear, probably during the first verse of Bottom's song.

124   *plainsong* having an unadorned song (normally a noun; here used adjectivally). The allusion is to the cuckoo's repeated call, with its traditional associations of cuckoldry.

127   *set his wit to* use his intelligence to answer

133   *thy fair virtue's force* the power of your excellent qualities

136–8 *reason and love.* . . . See Introduction, pages 22–3, 28.

139   *gleek* make a satirical joke

146   *still* continually, always
       doth tend upon (that is, waits upon)

149   *jewels from the deep.* There was a belief that precious stones were produced on the sea-bed.

153   *Moth.* This is a normal Elizabethan spelling of 'mote', which may be what Shakespeare intended. But the association with 'Cobweb' may support the traditional spelling with the modern meaning.

159–69 *Be kind and courteous.* . . . The repeated rhymes add to the lyrical effect of this speech.

161   *apricocks* (an old form of 'apricots', closer to the word from which it is derived)
       dewberries a kind of blackberry

165   *light them at the fiery glow-worms' eyes.* Dr Johnson tartly comments: 'I know not how Shakespeare, who commonly derived his knowledge of nature from his own observation, happened to place the glow-worm's light in his eyes, which is only in his tail.' (It is not certain whether Shakespeare intended *glow-worm's* or *glow-worms'*.)

174   *cry . . . mercy* beg pardon (for asking you your names)

178   *cut my finger.* Cobwebs were used to stop bleeding.

181–2 *Squash* an unripe pea-pod. *Peascod* is a ripe pea-pod. Compare *Twelfth Night*, I.5.148: 'Not yet old enough for a man, nor young enough for a boy; as a squash is before 'tis a peascod'.

187–90 *That same cowardly, giantlike Oxbeef.* . . . Mustard, of

143

course, is often eaten with beef. Bottom admires the patience of Mustardseed's kin in suffering this. By 'made my eyes water' he may mean both 'I have wept in sympathy with them' and 'they have made my eyes smart'.

193-4   *The moon methinks looks with a watery eye; | And when she weeps, weeps every little flower.* There was a belief that dew originated in the moon.

195   *enforcèd* violated. (The moon is Diana, the chaste goddess.)

196   *Tie up my lover's tongue.* This suggests that Bottom may (as he often does in performance) be making involuntary asinine noises.

III.2   Again there is no significant break between the scenes, in either time or place. However, this scene begins with a recapitulatory passage between Puck and Oberon. The end of III.1 would be an appropriate place for an interval in performance.

(stage direction) The Quartos read 'Enter King of Fairies, and Robin Goodfellow.' The Folio reads 'Enter King of Pharies solus' at the beginning of the scene, and 'Enter Puck' after line 3. The Folio is probably closer to stage practice.

5   *night-rule* actions (or possibly 'revels', amusements) of the night.

7   *close* private, secret

9   *patches* fools, clowns
    rude mechanicals rough working men

13   *barren sort* stupid group

15   *scene* stage

17   *nole* noddle, head

19   *mimic* burlesque actor

21   *russet-pated choughs.* The chough is a jackdaw. Its head is grey; but *russet* could mean 'grey' as well as 'reddish'.
    many in sort in a great body, in a flock

25 *our stamp*. Some editors, following Dr Johnson, emend
to 'a stump'. Fairies, it is argued, do not stamp; and
since Puck is alone, there is no reason why he should
use the plural 'our'. But Puck is the most robust of the
fairies; and 'our' might well be jocular.

26 *He 'Murder!' cries* one of them makes an outcry

30 *From yielders all things catch* everything preys on the
timid

32 *translated* transformed

36 *latched* 'moistened' (a rare sense) or 'fastened'

40 *That* so that

48 *o'er shoes* so far gone

53–5 *This whole earth . . . Antipodes. Whole* means 'solid';
centre, 'the centre of the earth'. The moon's brother is the
sun. *The Antipodes* means 'those who live on the other
side of the earth'. Hermia's notion is that the moon, creeping through the earth, will displease (by bringing night
with it) the noontide that the sun is experiencing among
those who live on the other side of the world. The
conceit is strained, no doubt for comic effect; but it has
its place among the play's other images of cosmic disorder, such as those in Titania's speech, II.1.81–117.

57 *dead* deadly

61 *sphere* orbit

70–73 *And hast thou killed him sleeping? . . .* This recalls
Hermia's dream that she herself was attacked by a
serpent (II.2.151–6).

70 *brave touch!* fine stroke! (ironical)

71 *worm* serpent

72 *doubler* (alluding to the adder's forked tongue, but also
including the meaning 'more deceitful')

74 *spend* 'give vent to' or 'waste'
misprised mood. Mood could mean 'anger'. *Misprised*
means 'misunderstood'. The phrase probably means
'anger based on a misunderstanding'.

78 *An if* even if
therefore for that

145

81   *whether.* This word seems often to have been spoken as
       one syllable – 'whe'er'.

84   *heaviness . . . heavier* (playing on *heavy* as 'sad, heavy-
       spirited' and 'drowsy')

85   *For debt that bankrupt sleep doth sorrow owe* (that is, as
       a result of the sleeplessness caused by sorrow)

87   *tender* offer
       make some stay wait awhile

90   *misprision* misunderstanding, mistake

92-3   *Then fate o'errules, that, one man holding truth, | A
       million fail, confounding oath on oath.* Perhaps: 'If so,
       fate has taken a hand, since for one man who is true in
       love there are a million who fail, breaking oath after
       oath.'

95   *look* be sure to

96   *fancy-sick* love-sick
       cheer face, look

97   *sighs of love, that costs the fresh blood dear.* It was be-
       lieved that a sigh caused the loss of a drop of blood.

99   *against* ready for when

101   *Tartar.* The Oriental bow was of special power.
       The image may have come to Shakespeare by way of
       Golding's translation of Ovid's *Metamorphoses*,
       X.686–7, 'she | Did fly as swift as arrow from a Turkey
       bow'.

104   *apple* pupil

113   *fee* 'payment' or 'perquisite'

114   *fond pageant* foolish spectacle

119   *alone* (probably means 'unique', 'unequalled' rather
       than 'in itself')

124   *Look when* whenever (a common Elizabethan use)

124-5 *and vows so born, | In their nativity all truth appears*
       vows being born so (that is, in tears) are certain to be
       true

127   *badge of faith* (that is, tears)

129   *When truth kills truth.* The 'truth' that Lysander now
       tells Helena destroys the 'truth' that he formerly told

Hermia. The truths conflict to cause a fray that is 'holy' because between truths, but 'devilish' because the truths are incompatible.

131   *nothing weigh* arrive at no weight (because the scales will be equally balanced)

136   *loves not you*. The interruption of the rhyme scheme is appropriate to the sudden change in situation.

141   *Taurus* a range of mountains in Turkey

144   *princess* paragon
      seal pledge

152   *gentle* perhaps 'noble' rather than (or as well as) 'kind' or 'mild'

153   *parts* qualities

157   *trim* fine (ironical)

159   *sort* 'quality' or 'rank'

160   *extort* torture

169   *I will none* I want nothing to do with her

175   *aby* pay the penalty for, atone for

177   *his* its

188   *oes and eyes* stars (punningly). An 'o' seems to have been a silver spangle.

194   *in spite of me* to spite me

197   *bait* torment

203   *artificial* artistically skilful (and, like gods, 'creating')

204   *needles*. *Needle* was often pronounced as a monosyllable – 'neele'.

206   *both in one key*. That two singers of one song should be in the same musical key is so obviously desirable that this phrase sometimes causes laughter. But the phrase 'voices and minds' in the following line shows that for Shakespeare the 'song' and the 'key' were distinct and that *in one key* means 'in mental accord'.

208   *incorporate* of one body

213   *Two of the first* (that is, bodies). *First* is a heraldic term, referring back to the divisions of a shield which have already been described. In the shield that Helena is imagining, the same quartering appears more than

147

once, but the whole is 'crowned with one crest' because
it belongs to one person.

215   *rent* rend, tear

225   *spurn me with his foot*. Helena had invited Demetrius to
spurn her (II.1.205).

237   *Persever* (a form of 'persevere', which in Shakespeare
always has the stress on the second syllable)

239   *hold the sweet jest up* keep up the joke

242   *argument* subject of joking

244   *Which death or absence soon shall remedy*. The exaggerated threat helps to preserve the comic tone.

247   *Sweet, do not scorn her so*. Hermia still does not realize
that Lysander is in earnest.

255   *withdraw, and prove it too* (that is, 'let us go and decide
the matter by duelling')

257   *Ethiope* (used insultingly – Hermia is evidently of dark
complexion; compare line 263)

257-8   *No, no. He'll | Seem to break loose, take on as he would
follow*. This passage is textually corrupt. The present
reading assumes that Demetrius scornfully says that
Lysander will seem to break from Hermia's protec-
tively restraining clutches as if to follow Demetrius to
fight with him, but in fact will not turn up.

258   *take on as* make a fuss as if (or 'act as if')

263   *tawny Tartar* (another exaggerated reference to Hermia's dark colouring)

264   *medicine* any sort of drug, including poison
potion (also could be used of poison; Q2 and F read
'poison')

267, 268   *bond* both 'pledge' and 'tie' (here, Hermia, who is
holding Lysander)

282   *canker-blossom* worm that cankers the blossom (of love);
or, perhaps, 'wild-rose'

284   *Fine, i'faith.* . . . Helena still thinks that Hermia is
joining in the men's derision of her.

300   *curst* shrewish, quarrelsome

310   *stealth* stealing away, secret journey

314   *so* provided that
323   *keen* bitter, severe
      shrewd shrewish
329   *minimus* tiny creature
      knot-grass a common, low-creeping weed. The juice
      of it was said to stunt growth.
335   *aby* pay for
339   *coil* trouble, bother
      'long of caused by, on account of
345   *This is thy negligence.* . . . The change into blank verse
      marks the change in speakers and tone, but the rhymed
      verse resumes at line 350.
      Still always, continually
350   *so far* at least to this extent
352   *sort* fall out
353   *As* in that
354–95 *Thou seest these lovers seek a place to fight.* . . . This
      conversation between Oberon and Puck is a turning-
      point in the action of the play.
355   *Hie* go
356   *welkin* sky
357   *Acheron* a river of hell, traditionally black. In *Macbeth*
      (III.5.15) Shakespeare refers to 'the pit of Acheron'.
359   *As* that
361   *wrong* insult
365   *batty* bat-like
367   *virtuous* potent
368   *his* its
370–71 *all this derision* | *Shall seem a dream and fruitless vision.*
      In the epilogue Puck suggests that the play may have
      the same effect on its audience.
373   *date* term, duration
376   *charmèd* bewitched
380   *Aurora's harbinger* the herald of the dawn; the morning
      star
382   *Damnèd spirits* the ghosts of the damned
383   *in crossways and floods have burial.* Suicides were buried

149

at crossroads. *Floods* may refer to those who have killed themselves by drowning, or to those who were accidentally drowned and whose souls, according to ancient belief, could not rest because no burial rites had been performed.

389   *I with the morning's love have oft made sport.* Some believe Oberon to say that he has often hunted with Cephalus, Aurora's (the dawn's) lover. More probably he is claiming that he has often dallied with Aurora herself. He is pointing out that he can stay up later than the other sort of spirits.

399   *Goblin* hobgoblin (that is, Puck himself)

400   *Here comes one.* In modern performances, artificial smoke is sometimes used to suggest the fog that Oberon has instructed Puck to cause (lines 355–7). But the scene can be equally effective if this is left to the audience's imagination.

402   *drawn* with drawn sword

404   *plainer* smoother, more level

417   *That* with the result that

421   *Ho, ho, ho.* This was Puck's traditional cry.

422   *Abide* wait for
        wot know

426   *buy this dear* pay dearly for this

439   *curst* cross

461   *Jack shall have Jill* (a proverb, meaning 'the man shall have his girl')

463   *The man shall have his mare again* (another proverb, meaning 'all will be well')

IV.1   At the end of the previous scene F has the stage direction *They sleepe all the Act.* This seems to imply that in performance there was some sort of a break during which the lovers remained on stage. It is unlikely that Shakespeare intended any break here. The lovers sleep

on stage during the scene between Bottom and the
fairies, unremarked by them.

In this scene Shakespeare mingles verse for Titania and
prose for Bottom.

1   *flowery bed*. It is possible that this would have been
represented by a piece of stage-furniture on Shakespeare's stage.

2   *coy* caress

19   *neaf* fist

20   *leave your courtesy* either 'stop bowing' or 'put on your
hat' (if the fairies wear hats)

22   *Cavalery* Cavalier (perhaps in imitation of the Italian
form, *cavaliere*)

23   *Cobweb*. In fact it is Peaseblossom who has been told to
scratch (line 7). Presumably this is a mistake of Shakespeare's. The alliteration seems intentional.

29   *tongs and the bones*. These were elementary musical in-
struments. The tongs were struck by a piece of metal.
The bones were two flat pieces of bone held between the
fingers and rattled against each other, as by Negro
minstrels.

Here F has a stage direction, *Musicke Tongs, Rurall
Musicke*. Music is not demanded by the line, but there
may have been some sort of musical comic business at
this point. Granville-Barker comments: 'The run of
the text here almost forbids any such interruption.
The only likely occasion for it is when Peaseblossom
and company have been dismissed. There would
be a pleasing, fantastic irony in little Titania and her
monster being lulled to sleep by the distant sound of
the tongs and the bones; it would make a properly
dramatic contrast to the "still music" for which she calls
a moment later, her hand in Oberon's again. A producer
might, without offence, venture on the effect. (But
Oberon, by the way, had better stop the noise with a
disgusted gesture before he begins to speak.)'

32   *bottle* small bundle

35   *thee new nuts.* Some editors make an addition (for example, 'thee thence . . .') to improve the metre. But as it stands the line gives most effective stress to 'new nuts', as a special treat.

36   *pease.* In Shakespeare's time this was both the singular and the plural form. It both means and sounds the same as 'peas'.

38   *exposition.* He means 'disposition', that is, inclination.

40   *all ways* in all directions

41–2 *So doth the woodbine the sweet honeysuckle | Gently entwist.* This has caused difficulty. *Woodbine* can mean 'honeysuckle' (II.1.251, and *Much Ado About Nothing*, III.1.30). Here it seems to mean 'bindweed', or 'convolvulus'. 'The honeysuckle . . . always twines in a left-handed helix. The bindweed family . . . always twines in a right-handed helix. . . . The mixed-up violent left–right embrace of the bindweed and honeysuckle . . . has long fascinated English poets' (Martin Gardner, *The Ambidextrous Universe*, 1964; Pelican edition, 1970, page 62).

48   *favours* flowers as love-tokens

53   *orient* lustrous

65   *other* others (a common Elizabethanism)

66   *May all* all may

68   *fierce* wild, extravagant

72   *Dian's bud* (the herb of II.1.184 and III.2.366). There was a herb associated with Diana, the goddess of chastity, and supposed to have the power of preserving chastity, called *agnus castus.*
      Cupid's flower (the 'little western flower' of II.1.166 and the stage direction at II.2.32)

79   *Silence awhile!* Presumably Oberon is simply urging his companions not to disturb the sleeping lovers and Bottom.

81   *these five* (the lovers and Bottom)

82   *charmeth* produces as by a charm

85   (stage direction) *They dance.* The dance is not merely an

added entertainment. Giving symbolical expression of the reunion of the Fairy King and Queen, it marks a turning-point in the play's action.

89 *prosperity.* Q2 and F, followed by some editors, read 'posterity'. At II.1.73 we have 'To give their bed joy and prosperity'.

94 *sad* sober, grave

96–7 *We the globe can compass soon, | Swifter than the wandering moon.* Compare Puck's claim to 'put a girdle round about the earth | In forty minutes' (II.1.175–6).

101 (stage direction) *Horns.* The horn was a signalling instrument, not used for music.

103 *observation* an 'observance to a morn of May' such as that mentioned at I.1.167

104 *since we have the vaward of the day* since it is still early. *Vaward* means 'forepart', 'vanguard'.

106 *Uncouple* release the dogs (chained together in couples)

111–13 *I was with Hercules and Cadmus once, | When in a wood of Crete they bayed the bear | With hounds of Sparta.* There seems to be no basis in legends for this statement, which presumably is local colouring.

112–13 *Crete . . . Sparta.* The hounds of both countries were famous, as Shakespeare could have known from Golding's translation of Ovid's *Metamorphoses* (III.247):

> *This latter was a hound of Crete, the other was of Spart.*

112 *bayed* brought to bay

114 *chiding* barking

117 *musical . . . discord . . . sweet thunder.* Theseus's acceptance of the yoking of opposites here anticipates V.1.60:

> *How shall we find the concord of this discord?*

119 *flewed* having flews, that is, the large chaps of a deep-mouthed hound
  sanded of sandy colour

122–3 *matched in mouth like bells, | Each under each.* The notion is illustrated by a passage from Gervase Markham's *Country Contentments* (1615):

153

> *If you would have your kennel for sweetness of cry, then
> you must compound it of some large dogs, that have
> deep, solemn mouths and are swift in spending, which
> must (as it were) bear the bass in the consort; then a
> double number of roaring and loud ringing mouths,
> which must bear the counter-tenor; then some hollow,
> plain, sweet mouths, which must bear the mean or
> middle part; and so with these three parts of music you
> shall make your cry perfect.*

It is unlikely that any pack reached Markham's ideal.

123   *cry* pack of hounds

126   *soft* 'stop' rather than 'hush'

134–5 *is not this the day | That Hermia should give answer of
       her choice?* Theseus had given Hermia till 'the next
       new moon' to make up her mind. See I.1.83–90.

138–9 *Saint Valentine is past! | Begin these woodbirds but to
       couple now?* It was said that birds chose their mates on
       Saint Valentine's Day (14 February).

140   *Pardon, my lord.* Presumably the lovers kneel, pro-
       voking Theseus's 'I pray you all, stand up.'

143   *jealousy* suspicion

162   *in fancy* impelled by love

166   *idle gaud* worthless toy, trinket. Egeus had accused
       Lysander of using gauds to attract Hermia (I.1.33).

172   *like a sickness* (probably means 'as in sickness')

188   *with parted eye* (that is, with the eyes out of focus)

190   *like a jewel* (that is, like a precious thing found, and thus
       of uncertain ownership)

191–2 *Are you sure | That we are awake?* This sentence is
       omitted from the Folio text. It is metrically rather
       awkward, and its omission may have been deliberate –
       whether on Shakespeare's or someone else's part, we
       cannot tell.

198   *let's.* Q2 and F read 'let us'. This regularizes the metre,
       and may be correct.

199   *When my cue comes. . . .* Bottom, too, is momentarily

lost between illusion and reality. As he awakes his mind goes back to the moment of his translation (III.1.95).

200   *Heigh ho!* a yawn, perhaps with a hint of 'Hee-Haw!'

203   *vision.* The word has been used by Oberon (III.2.371) and Titania (IV.1.75), and will be repeated by Puck (V.1.416).

205   *go about* try

207–8   *patched fool* a fool or jester wearing a patchwork costume

208–11   *The eye of man hath not heard, the ear of man hath not seen, man's hand is not able to taste, his tongue to conceive, nor his heart to report what my dream was!* The confusion of the functions of senses is used elsewhere in the play for comic effect (for example, V.1.189–90; and see Introduction, page 27). Attention has been drawn to the resemblance to 1 Corinthians 2.9 (Bishops' Bible):

> *The eye hath not seen, and the ear hath not heard, neither have entered into the heart of man, the things which God hath prepared for them that love him.*

213   *hath no bottom* is unfathomable; has no reality

214   *a play* (sometimes emended to 'our play' or 'the play'; 'a' is the reading of the early editions)

216   *her death* (presumably Thisbe's)

IV.2   With this scene we return to Athens.

4   *transported* 'carried off by the fairies' or (euphemistically) 'killed'

5–6   *It goes not forward* we're not going on with it. F reads 'It goes not forward, doth it?' It is just possible that Q's division into two sentences represents a deliberate pointing of the words.

8   *discharge* perform

9   *wit* intellect

11   *person* figure, appearance

14   *thing of naught* something evil

17   *we had all been made men* our fortunes would have been made

18–19 *sixpence a day*. This would have been a princely reward.

20   *An if*

24   *courageous* perhaps 'encouraging'; or perhaps Quince's blunder for 'auspicious'

33   *presently* immediately; very soon

34   *preferred* recommended, put forward

35   *In any case* whatever happens

V.1   This scene (which forms the complete Act) follows in the evening of the same day. Theseus, Hippolyta, and the two pairs of young lovers have been married, and come to a celebration.

This Act demonstrates Shakespeare's mastery of varied styles of both prose and verse. The verse in particular has great range, including the dignified and imaginative blank verse of the opening dialogue, the rather more familiar, somewhat humorous blank verse of Theseus's conversation with Philostrate, the many different measures parodied in the play-within-the-play, and the rhyming trochaic verses of the closing section.

(stage direction) In the Folio 'Philostrate' here and elsewhere in Act Five is changed to 'Egeus'. Philostrate's only other appearance is at I.1.11, where he has nothing to say. The Folio text seems to be economizing on actors. It seems desirable that the roles should be kept distinct.

1   *'Tis strange, my Theseus. . . .* These opening speeches are referred to in the Introduction, pages 33–4.

3   *antique* both 'grotesque' and 'old-fashioned'
      fairy toys idle tales about fairies

5   *fantasies* imaginations
      apprehend imagine, conceive

6   *comprehends* understands

8   *compact* composed
11   *Helen* (of Troy)
       a brow of Egypt a gypsy's face
20   *comprehends* includes
25   *More witnesseth than fancy's images* gives evidence of
       more than the creations of the imagination
27   *admirable* to be wondered at
32   *masques* courtly entertainments, centred on a dance but
       also having some dramatic content
34   *after-supper* the dessert, or 'banquet', of fruits and
       sweetmeats taken to round off the evening meal
39   *abridgement.* This may mean both 'a shortened version
       of a longer work' and 'something which will make the
       time seem shorter'.
42   *brief* short account, summary
44-60 *The Battle with the Centaurs....* In the Folio, Lysan-
       der reads the 'brief' and Theseus comments. This may
       well represent the practice of Shakespeare's company.
44-7   *The Battle with the Centaurs ... Hercules.* Theseus
       himself had taken part in a battle with the Centaurs at
       which Hercules also was present. The story is told in
       Book XII of Ovid's *Metamorphoses.*
47   *my kinsman, Hercules.* That Theseus and Hercules 'were
       near kinsmen, being cousins removed by the mother's
       side' is mentioned in the Life of Theseus in Shakes-
       peare's great source-book, North's translation of
       Plutarch's *Lives.*
48-9   *The riot of the tipsy Bacchanals,* | *Tearing the Thracian
       singer in their rage.* 'The Thracian singer' is Orpheus.
       The story of his being torn to pieces by the Thracian
       women under the influence of Bacchic rites is told at
       the beginning of Book IX of Ovid's *Metamorphoses.*
50   *device* show, performance
52-3   *The thrice three Muses mourning for the death* | *Of
       learning, late deceased in beggary.* It has been suggested
       that this refers to the death of some particular man of
       learning, variously identified. But there were many

complaints in Shakespeare's time of the neglect of scholarship and the arts, and it is not likely that Shakespeare refers to anything more specifically topical than this literary theme.

55   *sorting with* befitting

59   *strange.* Many editors have felt that emendation is necessary and have provided an adjective bearing to 'snow' the relationship of 'hot' to 'ice'. The passage seems perfectly satisfactory as it stands.

70   *passion.* The word could be used generally of any strong feeling, for example, 'idle merriment, | A passion hateful to my purposes' (*King John*, III.3.46–7). Its associations with grief as well make it appropriate in this context of antithesis.

74   *unbreathed* unexercised

75   *against* in preparation for

77   *I have heard it over.* When Philostrate heard the play is not a matter that will bear inquiry.

83   *simpleness* simplicity, innocence

85   *wretchedness* the lowly in both social position and intellect

91   *respect* consideration

92   *Takes it in might, not merit.* The meaning is clearly 'takes the will for the deed'. Presumably 'in might' means 'according to their capability'. The irregularity of metre suggests the possibility of corruption.

93   *clerks* scholars

96   *Make periods in the midst of sentences* (as Prologue is to do, lines 108–17)

104   *simplicity* sincerity, artlessness

105   *to my capacity* as far as I can understand, in my opinion

106   *addressed* ready

107   (stage direction) *Flourish of trumpets.* This direction is not in the Quartos. It comes from F, and probably represents the stage practice of Shakespeare's company.

108   *If we offend. . . .* Presumably Quince reads from a scroll. The comic device by which a bad reader reverses

the sense of what he is reading occurs in an earlier play, Nicholas Udall's *Ralph Roister Doister* (*c.* 1553, III.4). Quince's prologue is not in either 'eight and six' or 'eight and eight' (see III.1.22–4). Its form is that of a sonnet without the first four lines. Shakespeare uses the sonnet form for his prologue (or chorus) to *Romeo and Juliet* (Acts One and Two).

116, 126 *show*. This may refer simply to the appearance of the characters in the play; but it is quite likely that they should adopt attitudes or even perform a mime, in the fashion of a dumb-show, suggestive of what is to come.

118 *stand upon* bother about
  points both 'trifles' and 'marks of punctuation'

119 *rid* both 'rid himself of' and 'ridden'

120 *stop* in horsemanship, a sudden check in a horse's career; also the mark of punctuation

123 *government* control

125 (stage direction) *a trumpeter*. The trumpeter is mentioned in F, not in Q. He probably appeared in performances given by Shakespeare's company.

138 *hight* is called (an old-fashioned word in Shakespeare's time)

141 *fall* drop

143 *tall* brave

150 *At large* at length

152 *asses* (a subtly chosen word)

153 *interlude* play

161 *right and sinister* right and left; horizontal

161–2 *sinister . . . whisper*. The inexactness of the rhyme is of course part of the parody. An actor has been known to show Snout realizing the fault, and confusedly pronouncing 'whipister'. The effect was amusing. Shakespeare regularly accents 'sinister' on the second syllable.

164 *wittiest* most intelligent
  partition wall *and* section of a speech or 'discourse'

179 *sensible* capable of sensation

180 *again* back, in return

183   *pat* precisely

189–90 *see a voice . . . spy an I can hear my Thisbe's face* (another
       example of the comic dislocation of the senses; see
       Introduction, page 27)

190   *an* if

192   *thy lover's grace* thy gracious lover

193–4 *Limander . . . Helen.* Presumably 'Limander' is a mis-
       take for 'Leander', Hero's lover; possibly it is in-
       fluenced by Alexander, another name for Paris, lover
       of Helen of Troy.

195   *Shafalus . . . Procrus.* Mispronunciations of 'Cephalus'
       and 'Procris', a legendary pair of tragic lovers whose
       story is told in Ovid's *Metamorphoses*, Book VII. An
       English poem about them, by Thomas Edwards, was
       in existence by 1593 and survives in an edition of 1595.

200   *Tide life, tide death* come life, come death

203   *mural down* wall down. A conjectural emendation (by
       Pope) of a difficult passage. See the Collations, page
       170.

208   *in this kind* (that is, actors)

215–22 *You, ladies – you whose gentle hearts do fear. . . .* This
       passage (anticipated at I.2.70–78 and III.1.25–42) has
       provoked comparisons with an account of a happening
       at the Scottish Court on 30 August 1594. King James
       and his queen were celebrating the baptism of their son,
       Prince Henry, when a triumphal car was drawn into the
       hall by a blackamoor. 'This chariot should have been
       drawn in by a lion, but because his presence might have
       brought some fear to the nearest, or that the sight of
       the lights and torches might have commoved his tame-
       ness, it was thought meet that the Moor should supply
       that room' (from John Nichols's *Progresses of Elizabeth*,
       III.365). This is an interesting parallel with Shakes-
       peare's play, though not necessarily an influence upon it.

220   *fell* fierce (also 'skin')

233   *lanthorn* (a variant form of 'lantern', preserved here for
       the sake of the pun)

234 *He should have worn the horns on his head* (a waggish remark at Moonshine's expense; horns were the mark of the cuckold)

235 *crescent* a waxing moon

242 *for the candle* for fear of the candle

243 *in snuff* 'in need of snuffing' and 'in a rage'

250-52 *All . . . my dog.* Moonshine, in exasperation, lapses into prose.

255 *This is old Ninny's tomb* (indicating a change of scene. No further indication is necessary, though producers have been known to employ a tomb inscribed *Hic iacet Ninus*. Thisbe gets the name wrong again (compare III.1.90-91).)

266 *beams.* So Q and F; often emended to 'gleams', both to avoid the repeated rhyming word, and to fit the alliterative scheme. But 'beams' may be a deliberate comic touch.

270 *dole* cause of grief

277 *Fates.* The three Fates in Greek mythology were Clotho, who carried a distaff; Lachesis, who wove the web of a man's life; and Atropos, whose shears cut the thread when the web was complete.

278 *Cut thread and thrum. Thread* is the warp in weaving; *thrum* the tufted end of the warp. *Thread and thrum* means 'good and bad together'; 'everything'. The image is ingeniously related both to the fates and to Bottom's trade.

279 *Quail* overpower
quell kill

280 *passion* both 'suffering' and 'violent speech'

286 *cheer* face

299 *die* one of a pair of dice
ace a single spot on a die. *Ace* was near enough in pronunciation to 'ass' to justify the pun in line 303.

307 *passion* formal, or passionate, speech

310 *mote* (in early editions 'moth', a common spelling for 'mote')

311–12 *he for a man, God warrant us; she for a woman, God bless us.* This was omitted from the Folio text, presumably because of a statute of James I forbidding profanity on the stage.

315 *means.* To *mean* was both a dialect word meaning to 'lament' and a legal term meaning to 'lodge a formal complaint'. The legal term *videlicet* ('you may see') may suggest that both senses are felt here.

320 *tomb* (at this date, a true rhyme with 'dumb')

322–7 *These lily lips . . . green as leeks.* The parodic derangement of epithets here recalls the confusions of the senses in earlier scenes.

328 *sisters three* the Fates. This passage resembles the prologue to Thomas Preston's *Cambyses* (1569), a play of the kind that Shakespeare is burlesquing here:

> *But he when sisters three had wrought to shear his vital thread*
> *As heir due to take up the crown Cambyses did proceed.*

332 *shore* (that is, 'shorn' – a comic misuse for the sake of rhyme)

335 *Come, trusty sword.* In a comedy of 1607 called *The Fleire*, by Edward Sharpham, occurs the following passage:

KNIGHT *And how lives he with 'em?*

FLEIRE *Faith, like Thisbe in the play, 'a has almost killed himself with the scabbard.*

This appears to record a piece of comic business in early performances of the play.

336 *imbrue* pierce; stain with blood

342 BOTTOM. This speech is given to Bottom in the Folio, but to Lion (that is, Snug) in the Quartos. Shakespeare may have intended Snug to speak it.

343–4 *see the epilogue, or to hear a Bergomask dance* (a last touch of Bottom's characteristic verbal confusion)

344 *Bergomask* a rustic dance after the manner of Bergamo, in Italy

352   (stage direction) *A dance*. No distinct exeunt for the mechanicals is provided in the early editions. They obviously should leave after the dance, before Theseus's reference to their 'palpable-gross play'.

356   *overwatched* stayed up late

357   *palpable-gross* obviously crude

360   (stage direction) *Enter Puck*. Puck's entry is often made through a trap door.

362   *behowls*. The original texts read 'beholds'. The notion of wolves howling against the moon was proverbial; compare *As You Like It* (V.2.103): ''tis like the howling of Irish wolves against the moon'.

363   *heavy* weary

364   *foredone* exhausted

365   *wasted* used-up, burnt-out

371   *Every one lets forth his* each grave lets forth its

374   *triple Hecate*. The goddess Hecate ruled as Luna and Cynthia in heaven, as Diana on earth, and as Proserpine and Hecate in hell. Puck refers to her as goddess of the moon and night.

377   *frolic* frolicsome, merry

379–80 *I am sent with broom before | To sweep the dust behind the door*. Robin Goodfellow traditionally had the duty of keeping the house clean, and was often represented with a broom.

387   *rehearse . . . by rote* repeat from memory

390   (stage direction) *Song and dance*. Some editors believe that the song has been lost, with perhaps a separate 'ditty' referred to in line 385. Granville-Barker introduced 'Roses, their sharp spines being gone' from *The Two Noble Kinsmen*. The lines beginning 'Now until the break of day' are headed 'Ob.' in Q1. The Folio gives no speech-heading, prints the lines in italics, and heads them 'The song'. It is possible that these lines were sung, perhaps by Oberon, with a chorus of fairies. But there are objections. The lines are not particularly lyrical: Oberon is giving a set of instructions. Also

Shakespeare tends to differentiate his lyrics by writing them in a metre different from what comes before and after, whereas this is the same.

402   *mark prodigious* ominous, portentous birthmark

405   *consecrate* consecrated, blessed

406   *take his gait* take his way

407   *several* separate

413–28   *If we shadows have offended.* . . . These lines form an epilogue, addressed directly to the audience.

418   *No more yielding but* yielding no more than

423   *serpent's tongue* hisses (from the audience)

427   *hands* (that is, in applause)

AN ACCOUNT OF THE TEXT

A Midsummer Night's Dream was first published by Thomas
Fisher in 1600 in an edition believed to have been printed from
a manuscript written by Shakespeare himself. This edition is
known as the first Quarto. It was reprinted in 1619 in an edition
falsely dated 1600; this is the second Quarto, a reprint of the
first, with only minor differences. The play was also included in
the collected edition of Shakespeare's plays published in 1623,
known as the first Folio. Here it appears to have been printed
from a copy of the second Quarto in which some alterations had
been made from a theatrical copy. The alterations correct some
errors in the original text, and add some information about its
staging.

The edition closest to Shakespeare's manuscript, then, is the
first Quarto, on which the present edition is based. However,
like most editions of Elizabethan plays, the first Quarto was not
well printed. A modern editor is obliged to clear up inconsis-
tencies and correct certain errors made in the printing-house.
Some are extremely obvious. For example, at II.2.49 the first
Quarto has 'Nay god Lysander'. This is corrected in the second
Quarto and the Folio to 'Nay good Lysander'. Occasionally the
Folio happily provides a solution for a serious misprint in the
first Quarto. For example, at V.1.188 the Quarto reads, nonsen-
sically, 'Thy stones with lime and hair knit now againe'. This is
corrected in the Folio to 'knit vp in thee'. Other difficulties are
less easily solved. There are times when the Quartos and the
Folio make good but different sense, and the editor has to decide
whether he thinks the Folio's reading may reasonably be con-
sidered to be a correction of, or Shakespeare's own improvement
on, that of the Quartos. An example is at V.1.122 where the
Quartos have 'he hath plaid on this Prologue' and the Folio
'hee hath plaid on his Prologue'. There is very little to choose

between these two readings. There are also some difficulties which cannot be certainly solved. Examples are mentioned in the Commentary to III.1.75–7 and V.1.203.

The alterations made in the Folio which affect the staging of the play are slight but interesting. Obviously they reflect stage practice in Shakespeare's lifetime, or shortly after. One can see a real advantage to the actors in having V.1.44–60 broken up between Lysander and Theseus as in the Folio, instead of being spoken by Theseus alone, as indicated in the Quartos. We cannot tell whether such alterations were made by Shakespeare, or with his approval. The division into Acts is first made in the Folio. It is worth remembering that in writing the play Shakespeare does not seem to have had these Act divisions in mind.

A Midsummer Night's Dream is sometimes thought to have undergone revision after its first performance. This theory is connected with the belief that it was written for a special occasion. There is no certain evidence to support it. However, Professor John Dover Wilson, in the New Cambridge edition, brilliantly demonstrated that Shakespeare made additions to the play at the beginning of Act Five. Dover Wilson believed that the interval between the original composition and the rewriting was 'a matter of years rather than of hours or days', but this judgement is based only on considerations of style and is not universally accepted. The additions may well have been made during the process of composition. The demonstration depends on the fact that in the first Quarto some of the verse is printed irregularly. The following well-known passage (V.1.4–22) is printed here as it appears in the Quarto except that the disarranged verse is printed in roman type, and strokes indicate the true ends of the verse lines:

> *Louers, and mad men haue such seething braines,*
> Such shaping phantasies, that apprehend | more,
> Then coole reason euer comprehends. | The lunatick,
> The louer, and the Poet | are of imagination all compact. |
> *One sees more diuels, then vast hell can holde :*
> *That is the mad man. The louer, all as frantick,*

Sees Helens beauty in a brow of Ægypt.
The Poets eye, in a fine frenzy, rolling, | doth glance
From heauen to earth, from earth to heauen. | And as
Imagination bodies forth | the formes of things
Vnknowne: the Poets penne | turnes them to shapes,
And giues to ayery nothing, | a locall habitation,
And a name. | *Such trickes hath strong imagination,*
That if it would but apprehend some ioy,
It comprehends some bringer of that ioy.
Or in the night, imagining some feare,
How easie is a bush suppos'd a Beare?

The regularly divided lines form a consecutive passage, complete in itself. It appears that the lines in italics were written, perhaps in the margin of the manuscript, in such a way that the compositor was not clear how they should have been divided. Altogether there are twenty-nine lines, all at the beginning of Act Five, which seem to have been added.

The following notes record the points in the text of the play at which the present edition departs significantly from the first Quarto. Simple misprints, mislineations, and so on are not recorded. Quotations from the Quartos and the Folio are printed as they appear in those editions, that is, in old spelling and so on, though minor typographical differences from one edition to another are not noted. The more interesting textual points are discussed in the Commentary.

COLLATIONS

I

The following is a list of readings in the present text of *A Midsummer Night's Dream* which differ from Q1 and were first made in Q2, followed by F. Most of them are corrections of obvious misprints. (Q1's reading is printed on the right of the square bracket.)

I.1.   4   wanes] waues
II.2.   36   Be it] bet it
        49   good] god
        53   is] it
III.1. 50   BOTTOM] *Cet.*
III.2. 299   gentlemen] gentleman
       426   shalt] shat
IV.1. 127   is] (not in Q1)
       205   to expound] expound
V.1.   303   and prove] and yet prooue

2

The following readings in the present text of *A Midsummer Night's Dream* depart from those of both Quartos and are first found in the Folio. (The reading of the Quartos is given on the right of the square bracket.)

II.1. 158   the] (not in Q)
       201   nor] not
III.1. 76   Odours – odours! (Odours, odours, F)] Odours, odorous.
        81   PUCK] *Quin.*
III.2. 19   mimic (Mimmick F)] Minnick Q1; Minnock Q2
       220   passionate] (not in Q)
IV.1. 207   a patched] patcht a
IV.2.   3   STARVELING] *Flut.*
V.1.   34   our] Or
       122   his] this
       154   Snout] *Flute*
       188   up in thee] now againe
       342   BOTTOM] *Lyon.*

3

The following readings in the present text of *A Midsummer Night's Dream* differ from those of both Quartos and the Folio.

Most of these alterations were first made by eighteenth-century editors. Those that are of special interest are discussed in the Commentary. (The reading on the right of the square bracket is common to Q and F unless otherwise indicated.)

The Characters in the Play] (this list is not in Q and F)

I.i. 10 New-bent] Now bent

24, 26 ('Stand forth, Demetrius' and 'Stand forth, Lysander' are printed as stage directions in Q and F.)

136 low] loue

187 Yours would] Your words

191 I'd (ile Q1; Ile Q2, F)

216 sweet] sweld

219 stranger companies] strange companions

I.2. 24-5 To the rest. – Yet] To the rest yet

26-7 split: | The] split the

II.i. 79 Aegles] Eagles

101 cheer] heere

109 thin] chinne

190 slay . . . slayeth] stay . . . stayeth

II.2. 9 FIRST FAIRY] (not in Q, F)

13, 24 CHORUS] (not marked in Q, F)

III.i. 63 and let] or let

97 fair, fair Thisbe] faire, *Thysby*

118 ousel] Woosell

154-8 PEASEBLOSSOM . . . go?] *Fairies.* Readie: and I, and I, and I. Where shall we goe?

170-73 PEASEBLOSSOM . . . MUSTARDSEED Hail!] 1. *Fai.* Haile mortall, haile. | 2. *Fai.* Haile. | 3. *Fai.* Haile.

190 your more] you more

III.2. 80 so] (not in Q, F)

213 first, like] first life

250 prayers] praise

257-8 No, no. He'll | Seem to break loose] No, no: heele | Seeme to breake loose; Q1; No, no, Sir, seeme to breake loose; F. (The present edition follows C. J. Sisson's interpretation of this passage.)

258   he] you
406   Speak. In some bush?] Speake in some bush
451   To] (not in Q ,F)
IV.1.   40   all ways] alwaies
72   o'er] or
81   sleep of all these five] sleepe: of all these, fine
116   Seemed] Seeme
132   rite] right
171   saw] see
V.1.   191   My love! Thou art my love] My loue thou art, my loue
204   mural down] Moon vsed Q ; morall downe F
214   beasts in: a] beasts, in a
304–5   How chance Moonshine is gone before Thisbe comes back and finds her lover?] How chance Moone-shine is gone before? *Thisby* comes backe, and findes her louer.
362   behowls] beholds
409–10   (The second of these lines is printed before the first in Q and F.)

4

Stage Directions

The stage directions of the present edition are based on those of the first Quarto, though with reference to those of the second Quarto and the Folio. Certain clarifications and regularizations have been made; for example, at the beginning of Act Three, Scene One, the first Quarto has '*Enter the Clownes*'. The names of the mechanicals (or 'clowns') have been substituted. Also some directions for stage business required by the dialogue have been added. The more interesting stage directions of the Quartos and Folio that have been altered are given below in their original form. Also listed are the more important editorial additions.

I.1.   0   *Enter Theseus, Hippolyta, Philostrate, and Attendants*] *Enter* Theseus, Hippolita, *with others.* Q and F

15 *Exit Philostrate*] (not in Q and F)

19 *Enter Egeus and his daughter Hermia, and Lysander,
and Demetrius*] *Enter* Egeus *and his daughter*
Hermia, *and* Lysander *and* Helena, *and* Demetrius.
Q1

III.1. 0 *Enter the clowns: Bottom, Quince, Snout, Starveling, Flute, and Snug*] *Enter the Clownes.* Q and F

III.2. 404, 412 (Lysander's exit and re-entry are not in Q and F.)

IV.1. 83 (*to Bottom, removing the ass's head*)] (not in Q and F)

137 *Horns sound; the lovers wake; shout within; the
lovers start up*] *Shoute within: they all start vp.
Winde hornes.* Q; *Hornes and they wake.* | *Shout
within, they all start vp.* F

V.1. 0 *Enter Theseus, Hippolyta, Philostrate, Lords, and
Attendants*] *Enter* Theseus, Hippolita, *and* Philo-
strate. Q; *Enter Theseus, Hippolyta, Egeus and his
Lords.* F

107 *Flourish of trumpets*] *Flor. Trum.* F (not in Q)

125 *Enter Bottom as Pyramus, Flute as Thisbe, Snout as
Wall, Starveling as Moonshine, and Snug as Lion;
a trumpeter before them*] *Enter* Pyramus, *and*
Thysby, *and* Wall, *and* Moone-shine, *and* Lyon.
Q1; *Enter Pyramus and Thisby, Wall, Moone-shine,
and Lyon.* Q2; *Tawyer with a Trumpet before them.
Enter Pyramus and Thisby, Wall, Moone-shine, and
Lyon.* F

150 *Exeunt Quince, Bottom, Flute, Snug, and Starveling*]
Exit Lyon, Thysby, *and* Mooneshine. Q and F,
after line 152; F adds '*Exit all but Wall.*' after
line 150.

174 *Wall holds up his fingers*] (not in Q and F)

256 *Lion roars. Flute as Thisbe runs off*] *The Lion roares,
Thisby runs off.* F (not in Q)

260 *Lion tears Thisbe's mantle. Exit*] (not in Q and F)

352 *A dance. Exeunt Bottom and his fellows*] (not in Q
and F)

390 *Song and dance*] (not in Q and F)

MORE ABOUT PENGUINS
AND PELICANS

For further information about books available from Penguins please write to Dept EP, Penguin Books Ltd, Harmondsworth, Middlesex UB7 0DA.

In the U.S.A.: For a complete list of books available from Penguins in the United States write to Dept D G, Penguin Books, 299 Murray Hill Parkway, East Rutherford, New Jersey 07073.

In Canada: For a complete list of books available from Penguins in Canada write to Penguin Books Canada Ltd, 2801 John Street, Markham, Ontario L3R 1B4.

In Australia: For a complete list of books available from Penguins in Australia write to the Marketing Department, Penguin Books Australia Ltd, P.O. Box 257, Ringwood, Victoria 3134.

In New Zealand: For a complete list of books available from Penguins in New Zealand write to the Marketing Department, Penguin Books (N.Z.) Ltd, P.O. Box 4019, Auckland 10.

'It should be acknowledged now that the present RSC is a national treasure' – *The Times*

Formed in 1960 and now world famous, the RSC performs more Shakespeare than any other theatre company, at its theatres in Stratford – the Royal Shakespeare Theatre and The Other Place – and from its new London home, the Barbican.

Find out more about the RSC and its activities by joining the Company's mailing list. Not only will you receive booking information for all three theatres but also priority booking, special ticket offers, an RSC quarterly newspaper and special offers on RSC publications. You can also buy the Company's famous silk screened posters by mail order – we stock posters for almost all Shakespeare's plays as well as for the new plays and classics staged at the Barbican.

If you would like to receive details and an application form for the RSC's mailing list please write, enclosing a stamped addressed envelope, to: Mailing List Organizer, Royal Shakespeare Theatre, Stratford-upon-Avon, Warwickshire CV37 6BB. Please indicate if you would also like details of the RSC posters available.

THE TIMES SHAKESPEARE

The New Penguin Shakespeare series forms the basis of a unique new audio cassette adaptation of Shakespeare's plays, performed by leading actors and lasting approximately sixty minutes, called *The Times* Shakespeare. The cassettes are available from Ivan Berg Associates, 35a Broadhurst Gardens, London NW6. Each one costs £3.24, to include postage, packing and VAT.

The titles which are on cassette are:

HENRY V

JULIUS CAESAR

MACBETH

THE MERCHANT OF VENICE

A MIDSUMMER NIGHT'S DREAM

OTHELLO

ROMEO AND JULIET

TWELFTH NIGHT

More plays are in preparation.

SHAKESPEARE'S TRAGEDIES

An Anthology of Modern Criticism

EDITED BY LAURENCE LERNER

Shakespeare's tragedies have always been fertile areas for comment and criticism. The same dramas which inspired Keats to write poetry appealed to A. C. Bradley – or to Ernest Jones, the psycho-analyst – as studies of character; and where the New Criticism has been principally interested in language and imagery, other critics in America have seen the plays as superb examples of plot and structure. Most of Aristotle's elements of tragedy have found their backers, and – as the editor points out in his introduction – these varying approaches to Shakespeare are by no means incompatible.

In what *The Times Literary Supplement* described as an 'excellent collection' Laurence Lerner has assembled the best examples of the modern schools of Shakespearean criticism and arranged them to throw light on individual plays and on tragedy in general.

NEW PENGUIN SHAKESPEARE

General Editor: T. J. B. Spencer